THE WORLD CUP 1930 - 1982

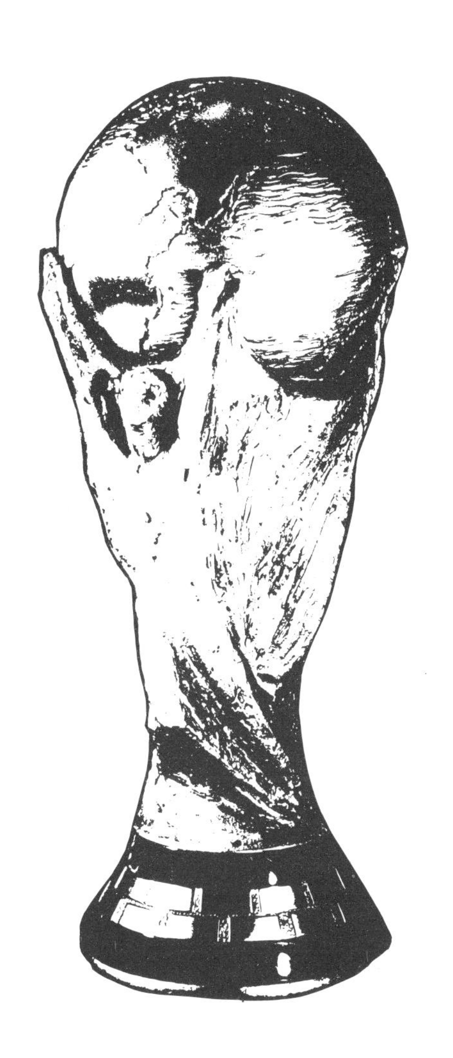

THE WORLD CUP 1930-1982

JIMMY GREAVES

Edited by
NORMAN GILLER

To Danny, Andrew and Michael, hoping you reach your goals in life.

First published in Great Britain 1982
by HARRAP LIMITED
19–23 Ludgate Hill, London EC4M 7PD

ISBN 0 245-53884-4

Designed by Michael Carter

Printed and bound in Great Britain
by Robert Hartnoll Ltd, Bodmin

Contents

URUGUAY . . . first World Cup winners in 1930.

Preface

A world-wide audience of more than 500 million television viewers will be switched on to the 1982 World Cup Finals in Spain from 13 June to the deciding match in Madrid on 11 July. This is an indication of the tremendous fervour and interest generated by the greatest Soccer show on earth – the World Cup.

In the following pages, we spotlight the players and the personalities, the matches and the moments that have made the World Cup on a par with the Olympic Games as the No. 1 sporting spectacle. My co-author Norman Giller and I have spent hours dipping into football history books and newspaper and magazine files to produce a comprehensive A to Z history of the tournament.

As well as factual and statistical information, we have unearthed a collection of amusing anecdotes and unusual happenings that we hope will make this book entertaining as well as enlightening. My own personal favourite story is of the player whose shorts came down as he took a crucial penalty in a World Cup semi-final. You will find a compilation of strange, curious and comical tales under the 'O' for 'Oddities' section.

I had the honour of playing in two World Cup tournaments – in Chile in 1962 and in England in 1966 (my contribution ended after the third match but I was as pleased as if I had been on the pitch when we beat West Germany 4–2 in the Final. Well, almost as pleased . . . !). My experience of World Cup competition has enabled me to give personalised assessments of many of the star players featured in the history section of the book.

Part Two of the book spotlights the twenty four finalists competing in the 1982 Finals. In my privileged position as a football analyst for Central Television and as a columnist for *The Sun* newspaper, I have been able to study video film and expert reports on all the teams and to help you get an instant evaluation of their potential I give each squad a star rating.

I sincerely hope you get as much pleasure out of reading the book as we have had compiling it. If it increases your enjoyment of the 1982 tournament in Spain, then we will have reached our goal.

Thank you for joining us. Now on with the Greatest Soccer Show on Earth . . .

Jimmy Greaves

ARGENTINA . . . World Cup winners in 1978.

An A~Z History

BRAZIL . . . outright winners of the Jules Rimet trophy in 1970.

ADEMIR, Marques Menezes (Brazil)

This quick, creative centre-forward reached his peak in the 1950 finals in Brazil when he was top scorer in the tournament with seven goals in six games. Born on 8 November 1922 in Pernambuco, a state in the north-east of Brazil, he started his career with his local club SC Recife. It was when he moved to Rio, first with Fluminense and then Vasco da Gama, that he established himself as a full international. Flanked by clever inside-forwards Zizinho and Jair, Ademir was a slim, moustachioed player who had the speed and explosive shooting power to turn half-chances into goals. He collected 32 goals in 39 matches for Brazil. His goals helped Vasco da Gama win the Brazilian championship without a single defeat in 1949.

AGE

Pele, at 17, was the youngest player to appear in a World Cup Final when he contributed two goals to Brazil's 1954 victory over Sweden. His fellow Brazilian, Nilton Santos, became – at 36 – the oldest player to win a World Cup winners' medal in the 1962 Final against Czechoslovakia. He also played for Brazil in the 1966 finals and won his sixty-fifth international cap at the age of 40. Mexican goalkeeper Antonio Carbajal was 37 when he played in the finals for a record fifth time in England in 1966. Stanley Matthews was 39 when he represented England in the 1954 finals. Obdulio Varela, at 35, was the oldest captain to lead a World Cup winning team when he collected the Jules Rimet Trophy on behalf of Uruguay in 1950.

ALBERTO, Carlos (Brazil)

Alberto captained the brilliant Brazilian team that won the Jules Rimet Trophy outright in Mexico in 1970. His adventurous overlapping runs from a right-back base were a feature of the Brazilian approach play, and his industry and invention were rewarded in the Final when he scored Brazil's fourth goal against Italy. Born in 1945, he became recognised as one of the world's outstanding defenders while a clubmate to Pele at Santos. He was skipper of Santos before following Pele's path to the United States where he became a popular player with New York Cosmos.

CARLOS ALBERTO . . . captain of the 1970 Brazilian World Cup winning team.

AMARILDO, Tavares (Brazil)

As understudy to the great Pele, 22-year-old Amarildo thought he was going to the 1962 finals in Chile just for the ride. But when Pele pulled a muscle in the second match of the tournament, Amarildo was suddenly promoted to the key position in Brazil's attack. He answered the challenge by scoring two goals against Spain in his World Cup debut. The reason he slotted so smoothly into the team was that he had his Botafogo clubmates Garrincha, Didi and Zagalo, to support him. Amarildo, nicknamed 'The White Pele', went on to help Brazil retain the World Cup, scoring the first goal in the 3–1 victory over Czechoslovakia in the Final.

COMMENTS

'I recall how relieved we England players were in Chile in 1962 when we heard that Pele would be missing the quarter-final match against us. Amarildo was an unknown quantity but we were well aware at the end of 90 minutes and after a 3–1 defeat that Brazil had uncovered yet another gem of a player. He was almost in Pele's class and there can be no higher praise than that. He continually confused our defence with clever changes of pace, passed the ball with exactly the right weight of contact and could shoot hard and accurately with either foot.'

ANDRADE, Rodriguez (Uruguay)

This coloured left-half completed a family double when he won a World Cup winners' medal with Uruguay in the 1950 Final. Twenty years earlier, his Uncle Jose had been in the Uruguayan team that won the first World Cup tournament. Rodriguez was a prominent player with Penarol, the famous Montevideo club, and his sound, authoritative defensive play earned him a recall to the Uruguayan defence for the 1954 World Cup finals.

APPEARANCES

West German centre-forward Uwe Seeler holds the record for most appearances in World Cup final tournaments, He played in 21 matches in a career spanning the 1958, 1962, 1966 and 1970 finals.

Mexican goalkeeper Antonio Carbajal is the only player to have appeared in five World Cup final tournaments. He was Mexico's last line of defence in 1950, 1954, 1958, 1962 and 1966, playing 11 matches.

Pele is the only man to have been a member of three World Cup-winning squads (1958/62/70). He scored in the 1958 and 1970 Finals but missed the 1962 Final because of injury. He played in 14 World Cup finals matches, two less than Brazilian record holder Nilton Santos.

Bobby Moore and Bobby Charlton share the British record with 14 World Cup final appearances each during England's campaigns of 1962, 1966 and 1970.

OSVALDO ARDILES . . . turning it on for Tottenham.

ARDILES, Osvaldo (Argentina)

This silky-smooth midfield schemer was one of the chief architects of Argentina's 1978 World Cup triumph. The son of a lawyer, he had to choose between law and football. He passed his law exams but elected to concentrate on earning a living with his feet and quickly established himself as one of the most accomplished players in South America while playing club football for Huracan.

Ardiles was 25 when he made the stunning decision to join Tottenham in a £325,000 transfer just weeks after helping Argentina win the World Cup. He has since won the hearts of all English football fans with his skill and sportsmanship.

COMMENTS

'He stood out in the 1978 World Cup finals as a midfield organiser who could dictate the pace and pattern of a match. I was pleased and astonished when my old club Spurs managed to snap him up but wondered whether he would settle to English conditions and the pressures of our overloaded fixture list. He has dispelled all doubts with a procession of high-quality performances that confirm his standing as a world-class player.'

VICTORS AND THE VANQUISHED . . . Bertoni, Kempes and Luque celebrate as the final whistle signals Argentina's triumph in the 1978 World Cup Final. Dutch goalkeeper Jan Jongbloed (No. 8) reacts with a gesture of despair.

ARGENTINA

Their full record in the World Cup final tournaments:

1930 France (1–0), Mexico (6–3), Chile (3–1), USA (6–1, semi-final), Uruguay (2–4, final).

1934 Sweden (2–3), Eliminated. Argentina left their best players at home because they did not want to risk having them poached by wealthy Italian clubs!

1938 Declined the invitation to compete after their bid to stage the finals had been rejected.

1950 Refused to take part because they were in dispute with host nation Brazil.

1954 Refused to take part following a continuation of their dispute with Brazil and also an altercation with Uruguay.

1958 West Germany (1–3), Northern Ireland (3–1), Czechoslovakia (1–6).

1962 Bulgaria (1–0), England (1–3), Hungary (0–0).

1966 Spain (2–2), West Germany (0–0), Switzerland (2–0), England (0–1, quarter-final).

1970 Failed to qualify following shock defeats by Peru and Bolivia.

1974 Poland (2–3), Italy (1–1), Haiti (4–1), Holland (0–4), Brazil (1–2), East Germany (1–1).

1978 Hungary (2–1), France (2–1), Italy (0–1), Poland (2–0), Brazil (0–0), Peru (6–0), Holland (3–1, final). Champions.

Summary: P29, W14, D5, L10, F55, A43

ASTON, Ken (FIFA referee)

Headmaster of a primary school in Ilford, Essex, Aston became one of England's most respected referees and was in overall control of World Cup match officials in the 1966 and 1970 tournaments. He was a tall, commanding figure who believed in taking firm control of games. Aston made worldwide headlines during the violent Chile–Italy match in the 1962 finals when he sent off two players. *(See Battle of Santiago.)*

ATTENDANCES

The biggest attendance for a World Cup match (and a record for any football game) was the 205,000 (199,854 paid) gathering for the decisive match of the 1950 finals between Uruguay and Brazil at the Maracana Municipal Stadium, Rio de Janeiro, on 16 July 1950.

The smallest attendance was 2,823 for the Hungary–Wales play-off in the 1958 finals. The previous day Imre Nagy, leader of the Hungarian uprising of 1956, had been executed and many people boycotted the game as a sign of sympathy.

World Cup attendances for each finals tournament:

1930 Uruguay 434,500 at 18 matches (av. 24,139)
1934 Italy 395,000 at 17 matches (av. 23,235)
1938 France 483,000 at 18 matches (av. 26,833)
1950 Brazil 1,337,000 at 22 matches (av. 60,772)
1954 Swiss 943,000 at 26 matches (av. 36,270)
1958 Sweden 868,000 at 35 matches (av. 24,800)
1962 Chile 776,000 at 32 matches (av. 24,250)
1966 England 1,614,677 at 32 matches (av. 50,458)
1970 Mexico 1,673,975 at 32 matches (av. 52,312)
1974 W.Germ 1,774,022 at 38 matches (av. 46,685)
1978 Argtne 1,610,215 at 38 matches (av. 42,374)

AUSTRALIA

Australia qualified for the World Cup finals for the one and only time in 1974. They were eliminated after defeats by East Germany (0–2) and West Germany (0–3) and an honourable goalless draw with Chile. They were coached by Yugoslav Rale Rasic.

AUSTRIA

Their full record in the World Cup final tournaments:

1934 France (3–2), Hungary (2–1), Italy (0–1, semi-final), Germany (2–3). Finished fourth.

1954 Scotland (1–0), Czechoslovakia (5–0), Switzerland (7–5), West Germany (1–6, semi-final), Uruguay (3–1). Finished third.

1958 Brazil (0–3), Russia (0–2), England (2–2).

1978 Spain (2–1), Sweden (1–0), Brazil (0–1), Holland (1–5), Italy (0–1), West Germany (3–2).

The Austrians did not enter in 1962 and failed to qualify in 1966, 1970 and 1974.

Summary: P18 W9 D1 L8 F33 A36

BALL, Alan (England)

Playing the game of his life, Ball helped push England to extra-time victory over West Germany in the 1966 World Cup Final at Wembley. At 21, he was the 'baby' of the England team and he gave Germany's Italian-based left-back, Karl-Heinz Schnellinger, a chasing he will never forget.

A red-headed terrier of a player, Ball has been the midfield motivator for Blackpool, Everton, Arsenal

ALAN BALL . . . 'Baby of England's triumphant 1966 World Cup team'.

and Southampton but it is for his exploits with England that he will be best remembered. This son of an ex-professional footballer was born at Farnworth, Lancashire, on 5 May 1945. He won 72 caps, skippered England six times and played in four World Cup final matches in 1966 and four more in 1970, including an appearance as substitute against Czechoslovakia.

COMMENTS

'I remember Ballie muttering darkly about going home when Alf Ramsey left him out of the England team after the opening 1966 World Cup match against Uruguay. But he was sensible enough to stay with the squad and became a hero in the Final when he produced mind-boggling energy to go with his considerable skill. What a competitor!'

BANKS, Gordon (England)

Rivalling Russia's legendary Lev Yashin as the greatest goalkeeper ever to play World Cup football, in 1966 Banks equalled the record of conceding only three goals in a full span of World Cup final matches *(see Goalkeepers)*. His save from a downward header by Pele in the 1970 tournament is still talked about as the finest reaction save ever witnessed.

Banks, born in Sheffield on 30 December 1937, played a record 73 times for England from 1963 until 1972, when tragically he lost the sight of his right eye in a car crash. The opposition failed to put the ball past him in 35 of his England appearances. He conceded only four goals in nine World Cup final matches, missing the 1970 quarter-final against West Germany because of a mystery stomach ailment. England's chances of retaining the Cup virtually disappeared with him.

COMMENTS

'If there has been a greater goalkeeper then I've not seen him. I know that Pele shares my opinion and no wonder when you consider the save he made against him in the 1970 World Cup. It was out of this world. There has been nobody as safe as the Banks of England.'

BATTLE OF BERNE

It was more like a war than a football match when Hungary and Brazil collided in the 1954 quarter-finals in Berne. The game was continually spilling over with violence from the moment in the third minute when Hungarian centre-forward Nandor Hidegkuti had his shorts ripped off him as he lashed a rising shot into the roof of the Brazilian net. Five minutes later, Hidegkuti centred for Sandor Kocsis to head in a second goal as cascading rain threatened to swamp the ground.

The tackling, particularly by the Brazilians, became reckless and ferocious. Djalma Santos pulled Brazil back into the game with a penalty but early in the second half Mihaly Santos restored Hungary's two-goal lead, again from the penalty spot.

Botelho Julinho made it 3–2 with a stunning shot after a weaving run through the Hungarian defence. Now the game developed into a wild brawl and English referee Arthur ('It's A Knockout') Ellis sent off Nilton Santos and Hungarian MP Josef Bozsik for having a fist fight.

Ellis summoned police to clear the pitch when the Brazilian trainer came on to argue with him, followed by a posse of Press photographers. There were personal feuds being fought all over the pitch and Brazil inside-left Humberto Tozzi fell to his knees pleading and crying when he became the third player to be sent off.

Three minutes from the final whistle Kocsis rose to head his second goal of the game to clinch a 4–2 victory for Hungary. But it did not end there. The fighting continued in the dressing-room with players of both sides being cut and gashed by broken bottles.

BATTLE OF BORDEAUX

The Czechoslovakian and Brazilian dressing-rooms resembled casualty clearing stations after a bitterly-fought 1–1 draw in the 1938 quarter-final at Bordeaux. The match marked the inauguration of the new municipal stadium. Scarred might be a better description.

Czech inside-left Oldrich Nejedly was taken to hospital with a broken leg. He was followed by a team-mate, goalkeeper Frantisek Planicka, nursing a fractured arm. Hungarian referee Paul Hertza sent off three players: Machados and Zeze of Brazil and Czech Jan Riha. At least six other players could have followed them as football took second place to fighting. Czech right-half Jozef Kostalek was badly injured by a kick in the stomach and three of the Brazilians hobbled off at the end of extra-time.

Brazil demanded that they be awarded the match but a replay was ordered just 48 hours later. There were no fewer than 15 new players in the re-match, which Brazil won peaceably 2–1, with French referee Georges Capedeville having no problems.

BATTLE OF SANTIAGO

Chile's players went into their 1962 World Cup match against Italy incensed by articles by Italian journalists that they considered an insult to their country. They took their anger out on the Italian players and the match, refereed by England's Ken Aston, quickly developed into an ugly brawl. Neither Aston nor his two linesmen saw a left-hook from Chile's Leonel Sanchez (the son of a professional boxer) that broke Italian Humberto Maschio's nose. Millions watching the match on television *did* see the punch and knew that the game was getting out of control.

Sanchez stayed on the pitch but two Italians were not so lucky. First, winger Ferrini was sent off following a clash with Chilian striker Honorino Landa, a decision he disputed for fully five minutes. Then full-back Mario David, aiming a revenge kick at 'boxer' Sanchez, was dismissed.

The nine Italian players left, including the injured Maschio, held out gallantly but were finally beaten by two late goals. Both teams and the beleaguered Ken Aston were escorted off at the end by a platoon of baton-waving policemen.

BECKENBAUER, Franz (West Germany)

FRANZ BECKENBAUER... 'stylish and as upright as a guardsman.'

Now winding down his distinguished career in Hamburg after a spell in the United States with New York Cosmos, Franz Beckenbauer will always be associated with the great Bayern Munich and West German international teams of the 1970s. He brought a new dimension to football with his attacking play from a sweeper-base at the back of the defence.

An elegant and inventive player, he captained West Germany to the Nations Cup triumph of 1972 and their World Cup Final victory in 1974. He was also skipper of the Bayern team that captured the European Cup for three successive years from 1974.

His 103 international appearances included the World Cup campaigns of 1966 (runner-up), 1970 (semi-finalist) and 1974 (winning captain). He bravely played on in the memorable 1970 semi-final against Italy despite a painful shoulder injury. He was voted European Footballer of the Year in 1972.

COMMENTS

'Stylish and as upright as a guardsman, Beckenbauer had marvellous vision and is the only player I would put on a par with Bobby Moore for being able to read situations and always take the right action. Understandably, he is known as "Kaiser Franz" in Germany and is certainly a king among players.'

BELGIUM

Their full record in World Cup final tournaments:

1934 USA (0–3), Paraguay (0–1).

1934 Germany (2–5). Eliminated.

1938 France (1–3). Eliminated.

1954 England (4–4), Italy (1–4).

1970 Salvador (3–0), Russia (1–4), Mexico (0–1).

Summary: P9 W1 D1 L7 F12 A25

BELLINI, Hilderaldo Luiz (Brazil)

Centre-half and captain of the Brazil team that won the World Cup for the first time in 1958, Bellini was a powerfully built defender who was equally efficient in any of the back-line positions. Born in Itapira, Sao Paulo State, on 7 June 1930, he was a hard, combative player for Itapira AS, Vasco da Gama and then Sao Paulo. He was 27 before he made his international debut but then his progress was rapid and within a year of winning his first cap he was leading Brazil to their first World Cup Final triumph. He was in the 1962 squad as a reserve full-back.

BERGMARK, Orvar (Sweden)

Bergmark was a solid and thoughtful right-back whose playing career reached its peak in 1958 when he played for Sweden against Brazil in the World Cup Final in Stockholm. It was one of 94 international appearances he made for Sweden. Twelve years later, in his new role as manager, he led Sweden to the 1970 finals after winning a qualifying group that included hot favourites France.

BOLIVIA

Little Bolivia have twice been invited into the World Cup finals in a football history that has been about taking part rather than winning. Each time they must have wondered if their journey had been really necessary. In 1930 they were hammered 4–0 by Yugoslavia and then 4–0 by Brazil. They were even more harshly treated in 1950, taking an 8–0 hiding from Uruguay.

BOZSIK, Josef (Hungary)

Born in 1925, Bozsik was an attacking wing-half in the 'Magical Magyars' team that won the Olympic title in 1952, thrashed England 6–3 at Wembley in 1953 and finished runners-up to West Germany in the 1954 World Cup Final, a match they were expected to win in a canter.

Bozsik, a member of the Hungarian House of Representatives, played 100 times for Hungary between 1947 and 1962, and his flair and fire provided an important midfield motivating force both for Hungary and for Honved, which he joined in 1937 when they were known as Kispest. After his retirement he continued to serve Honved as a coach and advisor until his death in 1978 on the eve of the World Cup finals.

BRAZIL

Their full record in World Cup final tournaments:

1930 Yugoslavia (1–2), Bolivia (4–0).

1934 Spain (1–3). Eliminated.

1938 Poland (6–5), Czechoslovakia (1–1, replay 2–1), Italy (1–2, semi-final), Sweden (4–2). Finished third.

1950 Mexico (4–0), Switzerland (2–2), Yugoslavia (2–0), Sweden (7–1), Spain (6–1), Uruguay (1–2). Runners-up.

1954 Mexico (5–0), Yugoslavia (1–1), Hungary (2–4).

1958 Austria (3–0), England (0–0), Russia (2–0), Wales (1–0), France (5–2), Sweden (5–2, final). Champions.

1962 Mexico (2–0), Czechoslovakia (0–0), Spain (2–1), England (3–1), Chile (4–2), Czechoslovakia (3–1, final). Champions.

1966 Bulgaria (2–0), Hungary (1–3), Portugal (1–3).

1970 Czechoslovakia (4–1), England (1–0), Romania (3–2), Peru (4–2), Uruguay (3–1), Italy (4–1, final). Champions.

1974 Yugoslavia (0–0), Scotland (0–0), Zaire (3–0), East Germany (1–0), Argentina (2–1), Holland (0–2), Poland (0–1). Finished fourth.

1978 Sweden (1–1), Spain (0–0), Austria (1–0), Peru (3–0), Argentina (0–0), Poland (3–1), Italy (2–1). Finished third.

Summary: P52 W33 D10 L9 F119 A56

Brazil is the only country to have appeared in all 11 final stages. They won the original World Cup trophy, the Jules Rimet Trophy, outright in 1970 after winning the championship for a third time.

PAUL BREITNER (West Germany)

One of the most inventive full-backs of modern times, this highly individualistic character established himself as a world star with Bayern Munich and West Germany, and later flourished his artistic talent in midfield for Real Madrid before returning

Carlos Alberto slides into a tackle to prevent Italy's Sandro Mazzola from making progress in the 1970 World Cup Final.

PAUL BREITNER . . . a one-off in the world of football.

to Bayern as captain and resuming his international career. Breitner will be a key man in the 1982 finals in Spain, marshalling the West German attacking force from a midfield command post.

He was born in Bavaria on 5 September 1951 and first came to international prominence when helping West Germany win the Nations Cup in 1972. His attacking runs down the left flank from his base at left-back were a feature of West Germany's 1974 World Cup triumph when his contribution included three crucial goals. Off the pitch, he is an intelligent and independent-minded person who preaches Maoist policies. He adopted a Vietnamese orphan and has worked extensively with handicapped children. Paul Breitner is a one-off in the world of football.

BROTHERS

There have been several instances of brothers who, relatively speaking, have starred for World Cup teams. They include:

Fritz and Otmar Walter, attack partners in the championship-winning 1954 West German team. They scored two goals each in the semi-final victory against Austria.

Bobby and Jack Charlton, key players in England's 1966 World Cup-winning team.

Twins Rene and Willy Van der Kerkhof, members of the Holland team that finished runners-up in the 1978 Final. Each scored in the eighty-third minute of matches against West Germany and Austria!

Other brotherly World Cup double acts: Juan and Mario Evaristo (Argentina, 1930); Fernando and Manuel Rosas (Mexico, 1930); Zlato and Zeljko Cajkovski (Yugoslavia, 1950); Albert and Robert Koerner (Austria, 1954); John and Eddie Souza (USA, 1950); Antonio and Francesco Lopez (Paraguay, 1950); Anatoliy and Viktor Ivanov (Russia, 1958); Piotyr and Emil Kozlicek (Austria, 1958); John and Mel Charles (Wales, 1958).

BULGARIA

Their full record in World Cup final tournaments:

1962 Argentina (0–1), Hungary (1–6), England (0–0).

1966 Brazil (0–2), Portugal (0–3), Hungary (1–3).

1970 Peru (2–3), West Germany (2–5). Morocco (1–1).

1974 Sweden (0–0), Uruguay (1–1), Holland (1–4).

Summary: P12 W0 D4 L8 F9 A29

CAPTAINS

The eleven captains who have collected the World Cup are:

1930 Jose Nasazzi (Uruguay), right-back.

1934 Giampiero Combi (Italy), goalkeeper.

1938 Guiseppe Meazza (Italy), inside-forward.

1950 Obdulio Varela (Uruguay), centre-half.

1954 Fritz Walter (West Germany), inside-forward.

1958 Hilderaldo Bellini (Brazil), centre-half.

1962 Ramos de Oliveira Maura (Brazil), centre-half.

1966 Bobby Moore (England), central defender.

1970 Carlos Alberto (Brazil), right-back.

1974 Franz Beckenbauer (West Germany), attacking sweeper.

1978 Daniel Passarella (Argentina), central defender.

The captains who have led Home country teams in World Cup final tournaments are:

1950 Billy Wright (England).

1954 Billy Wright (England), Willie Cunningham (Scotland).

1958 Billy Wright (England), Danny Blanchflower (Northern Ireland), Tommy Younger and Bobby Evans (Scotland), Dave Bowen (Wales).

1962 Johnny Haynes (England).

1966 Bobby Moore (England).

1970 Bobby Moore (England).

1974 Billy Bremner (Scotland).

1978 Bruce Rioch (Scotland).

CARBAJAL

This tall, agile goalkeeper made his World Cup debut for Mexico in the 1950 finals in Uruguay. Sixteen years later he set a record by playing in his fifth successive finals when he took over from Ignacio Calderon for Mexico's last match of the 1966 tournament against Uruguay at Wembley. In all he played in 11 matches, conceding 25 goals and finishing on the winning side just once. His most memorable match came against Czechoslovakia in the 1962 tournament. The game was played on his thirty-third birthday and he celebrated by helping Mexico pull off a shock 3–1 victory over the eventual runners-up.

Carbajal announced his retirement from international football immediately after the 1962 tournament but was lured back for the 1966 finals in England. His final appearance against Uruguay was a goalless draw, the only World Cup match in which he kept a blank sheet. The 37-year-old idol of Mexico then really did retire to concentrate on his glass-factory business.

CHARLTON, Bobby (England)

A non-playing reserve for England's 1958 squad after surviving the horrific Munich air crash, Bobby went on to play in three World Cup final tournaments and had his most satisfying moments in 1966 when he was a chief architect of England's triumph.

He was born at Ashington on 11 October 1937 and during his distinguished career won winners' medals in the World Cup (1966), European Cup (1968), League championship (1957/65/67) and FA Cup (1963). He scored a record 49 goals for England and was voted European Footballer of the Year and FWA Footballer of the Year in 1966. He captained Manchester United's 1968 European Cup-winning team, and shares with Bobby Moore the British record of playing in 14 World Cup final matches.

He played in all four matches in 1962 as an outside-left and had switched to a deep-lying schemer role by the time of the 1966 campaign, when his contribution to England's success, apart from a procession of precise passes, included three superbly-struck goals – two of them against Portugal in the semi-final. He set a then new caps-collection record of 106 in his final World Cup match against West Germany in the 1970 quarter-final, during which he was substituted before England's sudden nose-dive to a 3–2 defeat.

BOBBY CHARLTON . . . 'like a Nureyev on grass.'

COMMENTS

'Bobby was the greatest ambassador British football ever had. My outstanding World Cup memory of him was his performance against Portugal in the 1966 semi-final. He was the complete master that night, gliding across the Wembley pitch like a Nureyev on grass. It was a devastating show that frightened the watching West Germans into sacrificing Franz Beckenbauer as a marker on Bobby in the Final, a tactical error that played a big part in their eventual defeat.'

JACK CHARLTON . . . thanking a higher power for England's 1966 World Cup victory. ▶

CHARLTON, Jack (England)

He followed his younger brother Bobby into the England team as a dominating centre-half, winning 35 caps after starting his international career at the age of 29. Like Bobby, he played in all six of England's 1966 World Cup matches and, also like Bobby, his last international appearance was in the 1970 finals. He played in just one match in Mexico, replacing Brian Labone in the 1–0 defeat of Czechoslovakia. Born at Ashington on 8 May 1936, he played a record 629 League matches for Leeds between 1953 and 1973. He was Footballer of the Year in 1967, succeeding brother Bobby, and was elected Manager of the Year in 1974 after steering Middlesbrough back into the First Division. He later took over at Sheffield Wednesday.

COMMENTS

'Big Jack and Bobby were about as alike as grass and granite in personality and playing style. Jack's contribution to the 1966 triumph was every bit as important as Bobby's because he held the middle of the defence together, an important job for which there was no really suitable understudy after Maurice Norman had broken a leg and Peter Swan had been unluckily banned following the bribery scandal of the early 1960s. We called Jack the Giraffe because of his long neck. His power and command in the air was invaluable to England.'

CHILE

Their full record in World Cup final tournaments:

1930 Mexico (3–0), France (1–0), Argentina (1–3).

1950 England (0–2), Spain (0–2), USA (5–2).

1962 Switzerland (3–1), Italy (2–0), West Germany (0–2), Russia (2–1), Brazil (2–4, semi-final), Yugoslavia (1–0). Finished third.

1966 Italy (0–2), North Korea (1–1), Russia (1–2).

1974 West Germany (0–1), East Germany (1–1), Australia (0–0).

Summary: P18 W7 D3 L8 F23 A24

CLODOALDO, Tavares de Santana (Brazil)

An orphan, born in North Brazil on 25 September 1949, Clodoaldo made his international debut at the age of 19 against England in the 2–1 victory in Rio in 1969. A year later this strong and skilful Santos star emerged as a powerful force in midfield for the Brazilian team that carried off the World Cup for the third time. He scored a crucial goal against Uruguay in the 1970 semi-final and his linking in midfield was one of the outstanding features of the tournament. Clodoaldo was expected to be an even more influential player for Brazil in the 1974 finals but had to pull out at the last minute because of injury problems.

COHEN, George (England)

This quick and determined right-back brought strength and stability to the back line of England's defence in the 1966 finals with his powerful tackling and recovery speed. He had a long-running partnership with left-back Ray Wilson. They were a perfect balance for each other and they were among the first full-backs to operate the overlapping technique. George was born in Kensington, London, on 22 October 1939 and was a loyal servant to Fulham from 1956 until a knee injury ended his career in 1969.

GEORGE COHEN . . . perfected the overlapping technique.

COMMENTS

'One of the unsung heroes of England's 1966 World Cup success. George was so reliable in defence that he was often taken for granted and his adventurous right-wing runs helped no end in making Alf Ramsey's wingless 4–3–3 formation work so smoothly.'

COLUNA, Mario (Portugal)

This cultured midfield player won a record 73 caps with Portugal between 1954 and 1966. Like his Benfica team-mate Eusebio, he was born in Mozambique. He was the commander of the engine room in the Benfica team that reached four European Cup finals in the 1960s and under his quietly demanding captaincy Portugal reached the semi-final of the 1966 World Cup.

COLOMBIA

They have reached the final stages of the World Cup just once, in 1962, when they were eliminated after matches against Uruguay (1–2), Russia (4–4) and Yugoslavia (0–5). Their match at Arica against Russia in 1962 was one of the most sensational in the tournament. Russia led 3–0 and 4–1 but finished up clinging on desperately for a point after Colombia had battled back magnificently for a 4–4 draw.

COMBI, Giampiero (Italy)

He is the only goalkeeper to have captained a World Cup-winning team, leading Italy from the back to the first of their triumphs in Rome in 1934. Combi, who died in 1956 at the age of 54, made a nightmare start to his international career, conceding seven goals against Austria in 1924. But he showed 'unbeatable' form in subsequent matches and is warmly remembered as one of Italy's greatest ever goalkeepers. He won a bronze medal in the 1928 Olympics and helped Juventus win five League championships between 1926 and 1934. He was capped 47 times.

JOHAN CRUYFF . . . orchestrator of the Dutch attack.

CRUYFF, Johan (Holland)

Elected European Footballer of the Year three times, this Dutch master skilfully steered Holland to the runners-up position in the 1974 World Cup Final. Born within goal-kicking distance of the Ajax ground in Amsterdam on 25 April 1947, he developed into a stunning striker who could also scheme goals. He more than anybody was behind the Ajax rise as the kings of Europe and it was significant that when he moved to Barcelona in 1973 the Dutch team were suddenly not nearly the same formidable force. He was the orchestrator of the Ajax team that won the European Cup three times and he then inspired Barcelona to the Spanish championship. After a short retirement, he resumed his career in the United States and has recently returned to play in domestic Dutch football with Ajax, where he first made his name.

COMMENTS

'One of the truly great players of my lifetime, Cruyff mixed perfect technique and control with a flair that meant he was always looking to be inventive and imaginative. I recall a World Cup goal of his that captured just why he is rated a genius at the game. It was in Holland's match against Brazil in 1974 when they clinched a place in the Final. Rudi Krol fired over a centre from the left and Cruyff volleyed it into the net before the Brazilian goalkeeper had time to blink. Whether scheming or scoring, he was in a class on his own. I think Holland might have won the 1978 World Cup if he had bowed to pressure to make a comeback to the international team.'

CUBA

Cuba made their one and only appearance in the World Cup finals in 1938, accepting an invitation to compete after the Mexicans had withdrawn. They drew 3–3 with Romania and then won the replay 2–1 to qualify for the quarter-finals, in which they were crushed 8–0 by Sweden for whom right-winger Gustav Wetterstroem helped himself to four goals.

CUBILLAS, Teofilo (Peru)

This lion of Lima twice used the World Cup stage to show that he was one of South America's most talented and decisive forwards. As a young 'unknown' in Mexico in 1970 he had torn defences apart with his speed and explosive shooting power that brought him four goals in four matches. Eight years later, after a spell in Portugal, he returned to Peru and joined their World Cup campaign in Argentina. By then, at 29, he had developed into a more subtle all-round footballer, patrolling in midfield but still surprising goalkeepers with the velocity of his shots, as he proved with two stunning goals against Scotland and a hat-trick against Iran. He later flourished his skill on the USA circuit.

TEOFILO CUBILLAS . . . the Lion of Lima.

CZECHOSLOVAKIA

Their full record in World Cup final tournaments:

1934 Romania (2–1), Switzerland (3–2), Germany (3–1), Italy (1–2, final). Runners-up.

1938 Holland (3–0), Brazil (1–1; 1–2 in the replay).

1954 Uruguay (0–2), Austria (0–5).

1958 Northern Ireland (0–1), West Germany (2–2), Argentina (6–1), Northern Ireland (1–2 in a play-off).

1962 Spain (1–0), Brazil (0–0), Mexico (1–3), Hungary (1–0), Yugoslavia (3–1), Brazil (1–3, final).

Runners-up.

1970 Brazil (1–4), Romania (1–2), England (0–1).

Summary: P22 W8 D3 L11 F32 A36

CZIBOR, Zoltan (Hungary)

One of the 'Magical Magyars' of the 1950s, this quick and clever left-winger was mainly a maker of goals but also packed a cross-shot that brought him many vital goals for Honved and Hungary. He won an Olympic gold medal with the Hungarians in 1952 and switched to the right wing to help them take second place in the 1954 World Cup. On tour with Honved at the time of the 1956 Hungarian uprising, he decided to start a new life in Spain and joined Barcelona for whom he scored twice in the 1960 Fairs Cup Final.

DA GUIA, Domingas and Ademir (Brazil)

Domingas Da Guia was rated one of the most skilful full-backs ever to lace on a pair of football boots. He was a strolling player known as the 'The Sphinx' because of his expressionless face as he performed the sort of tricks with the ball usually the copyright of forwards. Never one to run if he could walk, Da Guia was a key man in Brazil's 1938 World Cup team that finished third. At times temperamental, he rashly gave away the penalty that virtually cost Brazil victory in the semi-final against eventual champions Italy.

Thirty-six years later, his son Ademir Da Guia made his World Cup debut for Brazil against Poland in the 1974 third-place play-off. Like his father, a powerfully built player, Da Guia showed that he had inherited much of the skill that made Domingas one of the all-time greats. Ademir settled into a midfield role and had a strolling style of play that conjured memories of his famous father.

DIDI, Waldir Pereira (Brazil)

Didi first brought his glittering talent on to the World Cup stage in the 1954 tournament, when he was a goal-scoring inside-right with prodigious skill. Later settling into a midfield role in a 4–2–4 formation, he was the brains of the Brazil team that won the World Cup in 1958 and again in 1962.

Football was an escape route from poverty for Didi who as a boy in the city of Campos used to sell peanuts in the street markets to help his parents make ends meet. An originator of the boomeranging free-kicks, he scored 24 goals for Brazil in 72 internationals. He was an idol with Fluminense and

DIDI . . . from peanuts to prosperity.

Botafogo but was less than popular at Real Madrid, a club he quit after only a short spell following a series of disagreements with another giant of the game, Alfredo di Stefano. As an attack-minded manager he steered Peru to the quarter-finals of the 1970 World Cup. He then coached in Kuwait before returning to Brazil as coach to Cruzeiras.

COMMENTS

'Didi was poetry in motion, a joy to watch even when you were playing against him. He always gave beautifully weighted passes and he could deceive the greatest goalkeepers with his viciously swerving free-kicks. Didi was particularly famous for his "falling leaf" free-kick. He used to put so much spin on the ball that it would hang and curl in the air like an autumn leaf falling off a wind-swept tree. He had slowed his game almost to walking pace by the time he faced England in the 1962 World Cup quarter-finals but he was still full of art and craft that put him a thought and a deed ahead of us mere mortals!'

DI STEFANO, Alfredo (Spain)

Surprisingly, this legendary centre-forward never played in a World Cup final series. He won international caps with his native Argentina and then moved to the then outlawed Colombia. But it was with Real Madrid that he moved into the land of football legend, scoring more than 500 goals for them, including 49 in 58 European Cup ties. He played in World Cup qualifying matches for Spain, scoring his one and only World Cup goal against Wales in a 2–1 victory at Cardiff in 1961. He travelled with Spain to the 1962 finals in Chile but was injured in a pre-tournament club match. It was suggested that he was fit to play but violently disagreed with the policies of outspoken Spanish team manager Helenio Herrera. A pity because the World Cup would have been a fitting platform for Di Stefano's stunning skills. Along with George Best, Di Stefano was the greatest player never to compete in the World Cup finals.

DRUGS

There have been two instances of players being banned from the World Cup finals for allegedly taking drugs. In 1974, a dope test on Haitian centre-half Ernst Jean-Joseph proved positive. He protested that he had to take the pills to combat asthma, a claim denied by his own team doctor. The distressed Jean-Joseph later claimed he was beaten up by Haitian officials before being flown home in disgrace. The following season he signed for a Chicago club.

In 1978, a dope test on Scotland's winger Willie Johnston proved positive. He had taken two Fencamfamin pills, first of all claiming he suffered from hay fever but later admitting it was something he often did before club matches. He was sent home and Scotland ruled he would never play for them again.

DUTCH EAST INDIES

Asia was first represented in the World Cup finals in France in 1938 when the Dutch East Indies accepted an invitation to send a team. But they found little joy at the end of their long journey. They were hammered 6–0 by Hungary in their solitary game but centre-half Alfa Meng created enough of an impression to get an invitation to play in Holland.

EAST GERMANY (German Democratic Republic)

East Germany created a favourable impression in their only World Cup finals appearance in 1974. They beat Australia (2–0), were held to a draw by Chile (1–1) and then conquered eventual champions West Germany (1–0) at Hamburg in the first ever meeting between the two countries. East Germany topped their qualifying group but did not fare so well in the second stage of the competition. They were beaten by Brazil (1–0) and Holland (2–0) and drew with Argentina (1–1). *(See Germany for the pre-1950 record.)*

ECKEL, Horst (West Germany)

Many good judges rated Eckel the key man in West Germany's World Cup-winning team of 1954 that scored a shock success over title favourites Hungary. He was a powerful right-half who mixed strength in the tackle with intelligent positioning and positive use of the ball. His excellent understanding with the famous Walter brothers, his Kaiserlautern clubmates, brought unity and organisation to the German team. Eckel retained his place in midfield for the 1958 World Cup but he was injured and failed to function with his usual 100 per cent energy as the Germans slipped to a semi-final defeat against Sweden.

EGYPT

Egypt qualified for the 1934 finals by beating Palestine. They had performed with credit in the 1924 and 1928 Olympics but were out of their class in the World Cup, losing 4–2 to Hungary in Naples. It was their one and only World Cup finals match.

EL SALVADOR

El Salvador's qualification for the 1970 World Cup in Mexico was achieved on the back of a full-scale war. They played two matches against their neighbours and bitter rivals Honduras and then won a deciding third game in extra-time. The viciously fought three-match serial fanned the flames of hatred between the two countries and within 24 hours of the third match they were locked in a war that cost hundreds of lives before a ceasefire was called. El Salvador were outclassed on the football field in Mexico. They conceded three goals to Belgium, four to Mexico and two to Russia without the satisfaction of scoring themselves.

ENGLAND

Their full record in World Cup final tournaments:

1930/34/38 England declined to compete and quit FIFA, the ruling body, following a dispute over broken-time payments being made to alleged amateur players. They rejoined FIFA in 1948 and qualified for the first ever post-war World Cup finals by winning the Home Championship.

1950 Chile (2–0). Williams, Ramsey, Aston, Wright, Hughes, Dickinson, Finney, Mannion (1), Bentley, Mortensen (1), Mullen.
USA (0–1). Unchanged team.
Spain (0–1). Williams, Ramsey, Eckersley, Wright, Hughes, Dickinson, Matthews, Mortensen, Milburn, Baily, Finney.

1954 Belgium (4–4, after extra-time). Merrick, Staniforth, Byrne, Wright, Owen, Dickinson, Matthews, Broadis (2), Lofthouse (2), T. Taylor, Finney.
Switzerland (2–0). Merrick, Staniforth, Byrne, McGarry, Wright, Dickinson, Finney, Broadis, T. Taylor, Wilshaw (1), Mullen (1).
Uruguay (2–4). Merrick, Staniforth, Byrne, McGarry, Wright, Dickinson, Matthews, Broadis, Lofthouse (1), Wilshaw, Finney (1).

1958 Russia (2–2). McDonald, Howe, Banks, Clamp, Wright, Slater, Douglas, Robson, Kevan (1), Haynes, Finney (1, pen).
Brazil (0–0). Same team apart from A'Court for injured Finney.
Austria (2–2). Unchanged team. Scorers: Haynes, Kevan.
Russia (0–1). McDonald, Howe, Banks, Wright, Slater, Brabrook, Broadbent, Kevan, Haynes, A'Court.

England's winning World Cup team parade the Jules Rimet Trophy after the 1966 Final. Left to right: Nobby Stiles, Jack Charlton, Gordon Banks, Alan Ball, Martin Peters, Roger Hunt (just visible between Peters and Hurst), Geoff Hurst, skipper Bobby Moore, Ray Wilson, George Cohen and a tearful Bobby Charlton.

1962 Hungary (1–2). Springett, Armfield, Wilson, Moore, Norman, Flowers (1, pen), Douglas, Greaves, Hitchens, Haynes, B. Charlton.
Argentina (3–1). Same team, except Peacock for Hitchens. Scorers: Flowers (pen), Charlton, Greaves.
Bulgaria (0–0). Unchanged team.
Brazil (1–3, quarter-finals). Same team, except Hitchens (1) for Peacock.

1966 Uruguay (0–0). Banks, Cohen, Wilson, Stiles, J. Charlton, Moore, Ball, Greaves, B. Charlton, Hunt, Connelly.
Mexico (2–0). Banks, Cohen, Wilson, Stiles, J. Charlton, Moore, Paine, Greaves, B. Charlton (1), Hunt (1), Peters.
France (2–0). Same team, except Callaghan for Paine. Scorer: Hunt (2).
Argentina (1–0, quarter-final). Banks, Cohen, Wilson, Stiles, J. Charlton, Moore, Ball, Hurst (1), B. Charlton, Hunt, Peters.
Portugal (2–1, semi-final). Unchanged team. Scorer: B. Charlton (2).
West Germany (4–2 after extra-time, final). Unchanged team. Scorers: Hurst (3), Peters. Champions.

1970 Romania (1–0). Banks, Newton (Wright), Cooper, Mullery, Labone, Moore, Lee (Osgood), Ball, B. Charlton, Hurst (1), Peters.
Brazil (0–1). Banks, Wright, Cooper, Mullery, Labone, Moore, Lee (Astle), Ball, B. Charlton (Bell), Hurst, Peters.
Czechoslovakia (1–0). Banks, Newton, Cooper, Mullery, J. Charlton, Moore, Bell, B. Charlton (Ball), Astle (Osgood), Clarke (1, pen), Peters.
West Germany (2–3, quarter-finals). Bonetti, Newton, Cooper, Mullery (1), Labone, Moore, Lee, Ball, B. Charlton (Bell), Hurst, Peters (1) (Hunter).

1974 Failed to qualify following defeat by Poland.

1978 Failed to qualify, finishing second to Italy in the qualifying group on goal difference.

Summary: P24 W10 D6 L8 F34 A28

EUSEBIO, Ferreira de Silva (Portugal)

Born in Mozambique in 1942, he was snapped up from SC Lourenco Marques by Benfica of Lisbon in

EUSEBIO . . . 'a man in a hurry.'

1961 and won the first of more than 60 international caps in his first season with his new club. Nicknamed 'The Black Panther', he could move through defences at sprint speed and had a tremendous right-foot shot that put him top of the Portuguese League scoring list seven times. He was voted European Footballer of the Year in 1961 and was the World Cup tournament top scorer in 1966 when his nine goals lifted Portugal to a semi-final place against England. He wound down his playing career in the United States.

COMMENTS

'Eusebio was a virtual unknown when I first played against him for Spurs in the European Cup semi-final saga against Benfica back in 1961–62. From my first look at him in action I knew he would be giving goalkeepers nightmares for years to come. The outstanding memory I have of him is a film shot of him in action against North Korea at Goodison Park in the 1966 quarter-finals. The Koreans had raced into an unbelievable 3–0 lead and then Eusebio took over. He scored four goals and I particularly recall the way he retrieved the ball from the back of the net after the first of his two penalties. That somehow captured the way Eusebio played his football. He was a man in a hurry.'

LOTHAR EMMERICH (No. 11) prepares to take the last-minute free-kick that led to the dramatic goal which forced England and West Germany into extra-time in the 1966 World Cup Final.

EXTRA-TIME

Three World Cup Finals have been decided in extra-time: 1934, Italy 2, Czechoslovakia 1 (score at 90 minutes 1–1); 1966, England 4, West Germany 2 (at 90 minutes 2–2); 1978, Argentina 3, Holland 1 (at 90 minutes 1–1). *(See Finals for scorers.)*

England have been involved in two other extra-time finishes to World Cup matches. In their opening game of the 1954 tournament against Belgium, England were held at 3–3 at 90 minutes and finished with a 4–4 draw. Then, of course, there was the repeat of the 1966 Final in the 1970 quarter-finals in Leon. West Germany pulled back from 2–0 down to 2–2 after 90 minutes and Gerd Muller made it 3–2 in extra-time. The Germans were then beaten in extra-time by Italy in a thrilling semi-final.

Both Northern Ireland and Wales qualified for the quarter-finals of the 1958 tournament after winning play-off matches in extra-time. Two goals from Peter McParland lifted Ireland to a 2–1 victory over Czechoslovakia. Goals from Ivor Allchurch and Terry Medwin brought Wales a memorable 2–1 win against Hungary.

FACCHETTI, Giacinto (Italy)

Italian Footballer of the Year in 1968, this tall, elegant left-back was an adventurous player who notched many vital goals for Inter Milan and Italy. He was born at Treviglio on 18 July 1942 and signed for Inter Milan at the age of 18, becoming a key member of the defence that stifled the life out of the best club attacks in Europe. His personal peak came in 1970 when he captained the Italian team that reached the World Cup Final against Brazil.

FIFA (Federation Internationale de Football Association)

FIFA is the ruling body of world football and was founded in 1904, with Belgium, France, Switzerland, the Netherlands, Sweden, Denmark and Spain represented at the inaugural meeting in Paris on 21 May. The main instigators were distinguished French officials Jules Rimet and Henri Delaunay, both men of great vision. The Football Association (founded in England in 1863) had originally suggested the forming of an international body but were not represented at the Paris meeting. There are now 145 National Associations in membership of FIFA. The possibility of a world championship was discussed at length at a meeting in 1920 but it was another 10 years before the idea finally got off the ground with the staging of the first World Cup tournament in Uruguay.

GIACINTO FACCHETTI . . . an elegant and adventurous full-back.

FEOLA, Vicente (Brazil)

A football academic, Feola was the manager of the 1958 Brazilian World Cup winners, prepared the 1962 champions and was back in charge of the squad that came to England for the 1966 finals. Ill health prevented him being present in Chile to supervise Brazil's 1962 World Cup triumph.

He graduated from the Sao Paulo School of Physical Education and trained the Syrian-Lebanese Club and the Portugese Club in Santos before, in 1937, starting an association with Sao Paulo FC that lasted for more than 25 years, apart from a brief spell of coaching Boca Juniors in Buenos Aires. A bulky, studious man, he treated soccer like a science and kept files packed with details of every international match he watched. He surrounded himself with a superbly well organised backroom team, including a psychologist and the intellectual Dr Hilton Gosling who had a diploma as a sports doctor and shared Feola's mania for detail. Dr Gosling visited 25 Swedish towns before deciding which area would suit Brazil best as headquarters for the 1958 finals.

Feola believed at all times in putting the *team* first, even to the point of threatening to leave the great Didi out of the 1958 squad because he was too much of an individualist. 'The job of the coach,' said Feola, 'is not to complicate but to simplify. The player is the coach's best friend, not some lump of plasticine to be modelled to the coach's whim.'

FILLOL, Ubaldo (Argentina)

This River Plate goalkeeper had been discarded by Argentina manager Cesar Menotti during the build-up to the 1978 finals but his consistent form demanded a recall and he became an important figure at the back of the World Cup-winning team. He is a steady, unspectacular player who takes great care to get his angles right. At 27, he was considered the one goalkeeper superior to the veteran Italian Dino Zoff in the 1978 tournament.

FINALS

This is a summary of each of the 11 World Cup Finals staged to date:

1930 Uruguay (1) **4, Argentina** (2) **2**
Montevideo, 30 July 1930. Attendance: 90,000.

Outside-right Pablo Darado shot Uruguay into a twelfth-minute lead but Argentina struck back with two goals in the last 10 minutes of the first half through right-winger Carlos Peucelle and centre-forward Guillermo Stabile. Belgian referee John Langenus turned away Uruguayan protests that

THE FIRST FINAL . . . Belgian referee John Langenus takes the eye as skippers Jose Nasazzi (Uruguay) and Nolo Ferreira (Argentina) shake hands before the kick-off to the 1930 World Cup Final in Montevideo.

Stabile was off-side when he scored. Pedra Cea equalised for Uruguay 10 minutes into the second half when he finished a spectacular dribbling run with an unstoppable shot. Left-winger Santos Iriate made it 3–2 to Uruguay in the sixty-fifth minute and reserve centre-forward Hector Castro clinched victory with a rising drive into the roof of the Argentinian net in the last minute.

Uruguay Ballesteros, Masazzi (capt), Mascheroni, Andrade, Fernandez, Gestido, Dorado, Scarone, Castro, Cea, Iriarte.

Argentina Botasso, Della Torre, Paternoster, Evaristo, Monti, Suarez, Peucelle, Varallo, Stabile, Ferreira (capt), M. Evaristo.

SEMI-FINAL Argentina 6, USA 1.
Uruguay 6, Yugoslavia 1.

Nine other countries competed: France, Belgium, Romania, Mexico, Chile, Brazil, Bolivia, Peru and Paraguay.

1934 Italy (0) **2, Czechoslovakia** (0) **1** *(after extra-time)*
Rome, 10 June 1934. Attendance: 55,000.

Thrusting left-winger Antonio Puc gave Czechoslovakia a shock lead in the seventieth minute. He had been off the pitch with cramp but came back on to take a corner and when the ball was kicked into his path he scored with a rising angled shot. Raymondo Orsi, one of three South Americans in the Italian team, equalised with an astonishing curling shot eight minutes from the end. The deadlock was broken in extra-time when centre-forward Angelo Schiavio raced into the middle to meet a cross from the right and steer the ball into the net in what was the ninety-seventh minute of a thrilling, evenly fought match. Fascist dictator Benito Mussolini presented the trophy to Italian captain Giampiero Combi.

Italy Combi (capt), Monzeglio, Allemandi, Ferraris, Monti, Bertolini, Guaita, Meazza, Schiavio, Ferrari, Orsi.
Czechoslovakia Planicka (capt), Zenisek, Ctyroky, Kostalek, Cambal, Krcil, Junek, Svoboda, Sobotka, Nejedly, Puc.

SEMI-FINAL Czechoslovakia 3, Germany 1.
Italy 1, Austria 0.

THIRD PLACE Germany 3, Austria 2.

Twelve other teams competed: USA, Romania, Belgium, France, Spain, Brazil, Switzerland, Holland, Sweden, Argentina, Hungary, Egypt.

1938 Italy (3) 4, Hungary (1) 2
Paris, 19 June 1938. Attendance: 45,000.

Italy took an eighth-minute lead when Luigi Colaussi slipped the ball smartly into the net after a brilliant 60-yard run by outside-right Amadeo Biavati. Just 60 seconds later Hungary pulled level when the unmarked Titkos scored from close range. But Italy were back in the lead after 15 minutes, centre-forward Sylvio Piola putting the finishing touch to neat approach play by captain Peppino Meazza. It was Meazza who set up a second goal for Colaussi 10 minutes before half-time. Hungary bravely tried to battle back in the second half and

Hungarian goalkeeper Antal Szabo dives too late to stop Luigi Colaussi's shot giving Italy an eighth minute lead in the 1938 World Cup Final in Paris.

their hopes rose in the sixty-fifth minute when Georges Sarosi scrambled their second goal. But Italy were always the superior side and Piola put the game beyond Hungary 10 minutes from the end when he scored with a powerful shot after running on to a neat back-heel from Biavati.

Italy Olivieri, Foni, Rava, Serantoni, Andreolo, Locatelli, Biavati, Meazza (capt), Piola, Ferrari, Colaussi.

Hungary Szabo, Polgar, Biro, Szalay, Szucs, Lazar, Sas, Vincze, Sarosi (capt), Szellenger, Titkos.

SEMI-FINAL Italy 2, Brazil 1.
Hungary 5, Sweden 1.

THIRD PLACE Brazil 4, Sweden 2.

Twelve other countries competed: Switzerland, Germany, Cuba, Romania, Hungary, Dutch East Indies, France, Belgium, Czechoslovakia, Holland, Poland, Norway.

1950 Uruguay (0) 2, Brazil (0) 1
Rio, 16 July 1950. Attendance: 199,854.

Strictly speaking this was not a Final but a deciding match of a final pool involving Uruguay, Brazil, Sweden and Spain. Brazil needed only a draw to take the trophy in front of a fanatical crowd and they seemed certain to be crowned world champions when right-winger Friaca shot them into the lead two minutes after half-time. But Uruguay, superbly marshalled by skipper Obdulio Varela, stayed calm and composed, and replied with an equaliser 18 minutes later by inside-left Juan Schiaffino. Then, with just 11 minutes to go, hurtling winger Alcide Ghiggia exchanged passes with his partner Julio Perez before crashing a winning shot into the Brazilian net.

Uruguay Maspoli, Gonzales, Tejera, Gambetta, Varela (capt), Andrade, Ghiggia, Perez, Miguez, Schiaffino, Moran.

Brazil Barbose, Augusto (capt), Juvenal, Bauer, Danilo, Bigode, Friaca, Zizinho, Ademir, Jair, Chico.

THIRD PLACE Sweden 3, Spain 1 (final pool match).

Nine other countries qualified: Yugoslavia, Switzerland, Mexico, England, Chile, USA, Italy, Paraguay, Bolivia.

1954 West Germany (2) 3, Hungary (2) 2
Berne, 4 July 1954. Attendance: 60,000.

Hungary, the 'Magical Magyars', were scorching-hot favourites to win and everything seemed to be going to form when Ferenc Puskas and Zoltan Czibor scored goals within 90 seconds of each other before the game was 10 minutes old. But the key man Puskas was not 100 per cent fit and Hungary began to look decidedly shaky under a series of swift counter-attacks by the brave Germans. They quickly pulled level with goals from Max Morlock and Helmuth Rahn and it was the powerfully built right-winger Rahn who shot the ball left-footed into Hungary's net for the winning goal 12 minutes from the end. Puskas thought he had snatched a dramatic late equaliser but English referee Bill Ling ruled it out after Welsh linesman Mervyn Griffiths had flagged for a disputed off-side. To the surprise of most people, it was German captain Fritz Walter who collected the trophy from the veteran Jules Rimet, retiring President of FIFA.

Germany Turek, Posipal, Kohlmeyer, Eckel, Liebrich, Mai, Rahn, Morlock, O. Walter, F. Walter (capt), Schaefer.

Hungary Grosics, Buzansky, Lantos, Bozsik, Lorant, Zakarias, Czibor, Kocsis, Hidegkuti, Puskas (capt), J. Toth.

SEMI-FINAL Hungary 4, Uruguay 2 (after extra-time).
Germany 6, Austria 1.
THIRD PLACE Austria 3, Uruguay 1.

Twelve other countries qualified: Brazil, Yugoslavia, France, Mexico, Turkey, Korea, Czechoslovakia, Scotland, England, Italy, Switzerland, Belgium.

1958 Brazil (2) 5, Sweden (1) 2
Stockholm, 29 June 1958. Attendance: 49,737.

Sweden took a stunning lead in the fourth minute when Nils Liedholm drifted through the Brazilian defence on a rain-sodden surface and scored with a powerful low shot. It was the first time Brazil had been behind in the tournament but Sweden's supremacy did not last long. Brazil, with their silky-smooth 'samba soccer', were soon 2–1 in the lead after the jinking Garrincha had created two goals for the explosive Vava. Then, 10 minutes after half-time, 17-year-old Pele scored a story-book goal. He caught a high, dropping ball in the middle of the penalty area on his thigh, hooked it over his head, whirled round the marking centre-half in time to meet the ball on the volley and send it crashing past Swedish goalkeeper Svensson. Mario Zagallo beat two defenders before shooting Brazil's fourth goal in the seventy-seventh minute and in the hectic closing stages Agne Simonsson pulled a goal back for the

A 17-year-old youngster called Pele puts Sweden's goalkeeper Kalie Svensson under pressure in the 1958 Final in Stockholm.

gallant Swedes before Pele put the finishing touch with a magnificent headed goal from Zagalo's centre.

Brazil Gylmar, D. Santos, N. Santos, Zito, Bellini (capt), Garrincha, Didi, Vava, Pele, Zagalo.

Sweden Svensson, Bergmark, Axbom, Boerjesson, Gustavsson, Parling, Hamrin, Gren, Simonsson, Liedholm (capt), Skoglund.

SEMI-FINAL Brazil 5, France 2.
Sweden 3, West Germany 1.
THIRD PLACE France 6, West Germany 3.

Twelve other countries qualified: Czechoslovakia, Northern Ireland, Argentina, Yugoslavia, Paraguay, Scotland, Hungary, Wales, Mexico, England, Russia, Austria.

1962 Brazil (1) 3, Czechoslovakia (1) 1
Santiago, Chile, 17 June 1962. Attendance: 68,679.
As in the 1958 Final Brazil were hit by an early goal, this time when powerful Czech Josef Masopust came running through from a deep position to convert a superb pass by Scherer into a goal. Brazil, without the injured Pele, quickly recovered from this fifteenth minute blow and were level inside three minutes as Amarildo, Pele's brilliant deputy, deceived Czech goalkeeper Viliam Schroif with a curling shot. It was Amarildo who created Brazil's second goal in the sixty-eighth minute when Zito headed in his cross. It was all over 13 minutes from the final whistle when the usually reliable Schroif dropped a teasing lob from Djalma Santos and Vava eagerly steered the loose ball into the net for his third goal in two Finals.

Brazil Gylmar, D. Santos, Mauro (capt), Zozimo, N. Santos, Zito, Didi, Garrincha, Vava, Amarildo, Zagalo.

Czechoslovakia Schroif, Tichy, Novak (capt), Pluskal, Popluhar, Mosopust, Pospichal, Scherer, Kvasniak, Kadraba, Jelinek.

SEMI-FINAL Brazil 4, Chile 2.
Czechoslovakia 3, Yugoslavia 1.
THIRD PLACE Chile 1, Yugoslavia 0.

Geoff 'The Hammer' Hurst unleashes the shot that completed his historic hat-trick and clinched victory for England in the 1966 World Cup Final at Wembley.

Twelve other countries qualified: Russia, Uruguay, Colombia, West Germany, Italy, Switzerland, Mexico, Spain, Hungary, England, Argentina, Bulgaria.

1966 England (1) 4, West Germany (1) 2 *(after extra-time)*
Wembley, 30 July 1966. Attendance: 93,802.

As in five of the previous Finals, the first team to take the lead eventually finished up second best. This time it was West Germany who scored in the thirteenth minute when a rare error by left-back Ray Wilson let Helmut Haller in for a gift goal. England equalised just six minutes later as Geoff Hurst glided in a header from a free-kick by West Ham clubmate Bobby Moore, who gave an immaculate display in the England defence. Martin Peters, a third West Ham player in the team, thought he had struck the winning goal in the seventy-eighth minute but central defender Wolfgang Weber scrambled a dramatic equaliser in the closing seconds.

After 100 minutes of exhausting football, the tireless Alan Ball found Geoff Hurst with a centre and his thundering shot struck the underside of the bar and bounced down. The Swiss referee awarded a goal after a Russian linesman had signalled that the ball had crossed the line. Hurst put an end to all arguments in the last minute with a crashing left-foot shot that completed the only hat-trick in the history of World Cup Finals.

England Banks, Cohen, Wilson, Stiles, J. Charlton, Moore (capt), Ball, Hurst, B. Charlton, Hunt, Peters.

West Germany Tilkowski, Hottges, Schulz, Weber, Schnellinger, Haller, Beckenbauer, Overath, Seeler (capt), Held, Emmerich.

SEMI-FINAL West Germany 2, Russia 1.
England 2, Portugal 1.
THIRD PLACE Portugal 2, Russia 1.

Twelve other countries qualified: Uruguay, Mexico, France, Argentina, Spain, Switzerland, Hungary, Brazil, Bulgaria, North Korea, Italy, Chile.

1970 Brazil (1) 4, Italy (1) 1
Mexico City, 21 June 1970. Attendance: 107,412.

Both Brazil and Italy had won the World Cup twice before and the extra incentive in this Final was that the winners would keep the Jules Rimet Trophy for all time. There was never any real doubt that it would be Brazil who would capture the prize. They took the lead after 18 minutes when Pele scored with a spectacular header from Rivelino's cross. Clodoaldo had a rare lapse of concentration seven minutes before half-time and back-heeled the ball into the path of Boninsegna who gratefully raced away to give Italy a surprise equaliser.

Brazil took command again in the second-half and schemer Gerson turned scorer in the sixty-sixth minute as he rifled in a left-foot cross shot from just outside the penalty area. Goals from Jairzinho and Carlos Alberto wrapped it up for Brazil as Italy made the odd substitution of sending on 'Golden Boy' midfield player Gianni Rivera to replace striker Boninsegna six minutes from the end.

Brazil Felix, Carlos Alberto (capt), Brito, Piazza, Everaldo, Clodoaldo, Gerson, Jairzinho. Tostao, Pele, Rivelino.

Italy Albertosi, Cera, Burgnich (Juliano), Rosato, Facchetti (capt), Domenghini, Mazzola, De Sisti, Boninsegna (Rivera), Riva.

SEMI-FINAL Italy 4, West Germany 3 (after extra-time).
Brazil 3, Uruguay 1.

Twelve other countries qualified: Russia, Mexico, Belgium, El Salvador, Sweden, Israel, England, Romania, Czechoslovakia, Peru, Bulgaria, Morocco.

1974 West Germany (2) 2, Holland (1) 1
Munich, 7 July 1974. Attendance: 77,933.

There was a sensational start to this Final, with English referee Jack Taylor awarding Holland a first-minute penalty before any German player had even touched the ball. The Dutch played a stunning series of 15 passes before Johan Cruyff made a dash for goal. He was tripped by Uli Hoeness and Taylor had no hesitation in awarding a penalty. Johan Neeskens coolly scored from the spot. Just as it looked as if West Germany were going to be paralysed by the strolling players of Holland they got back into the game and again it was a goal scored from the penalty spot, this time by Paul Breitner after Bernd Holzenbein had been brought down. Suddenly it was a different game, with Holland now on the rack under a series of raids from West Germany.

The pressure reached its peak in the forty-third minute when ace opportunist Gerd Muller swept the ball into the net for his sixty-eighth goal for West Germany. Holland, inspired by Cruyff but missing the left-wing magic of injured Robbie Rensenbrink, played some beautiful football in the second half but could not break down a German defence in which goalkeeper Sepp Maier was in magnificent form.

West Germany Maier, Beckenbauer (capt),

Goalkeeper Sepp Maier, shielded by skipper Franz Beckenbauer, stops Johan Cruyff from scoring for Holland in the 1974 World Cup Final but at a painful price.

Vogts, Schwarzenbeck, Breitner, Bonhof, Hoeness, Overath, Grabowski, Muller, Holzenbein.

Holland Jongbloed, Suurbier, Rijsbergen (De Jong), Haan, Krol, Jansen, Neeskens, Van Hanegem, Rep, Cruyff (capt), Rensenbrink (R. Van der Kerkhof).

THIRD PLACE Poland 1, Brazil 0.

Twelve other countries qualified: East Germany, Chile, Australia, Italy, Haiti, Yugoslavia, Scotland, Zaire, Sweden, Bulgaria, Uruguay.

1978 Argentina (1) **3, Holland** (0) **1** *(after extra-time)*

Buenos Aires, 25 June 1978. Attendance: 77,000.

In one of the fiercest of all Finals – scarred by more than 50 fouls – Argentina took a first-half lead through Mario Kempes in the thirty-eighth minute. Holland, missing the drive and invention of the absent Johan Cruyff, threatened to equalise seconds before half-time but goalkeeper Ubaldo Fillol made a crucial save from Robbie Rensenbrink. Holland scored the equaliser they were always threatening seven minutes from the end when tall substitute Dirk Nanninga headed in a cross from Rene Van der

Kerkhof. In the last minute Rensenbrink fired a shot against a post. Argentina had come that close to defeat but recovered in extra-time to take command and the new trophy with goals from the talented Kempes and Daniel Bertoni after a Kempes run had split the Dutch defence wide open.

Argentina Fillol, Olquin, Galvan, Passarella (capt), Tarantini, Ardiles (Larrosa), Gallego, Kempes, Bertoni, Luque, Ortiz (Houseman).

Holland Jongbloed, Krol (capt), Poortvliet, Brandts, Jansen (Suurbier), W. Van der Kerkhof, Neeskens, Haan, Rep (Nanninga), Rensenbrink, R. Van der Kerkhof.

THIRD PLACE Brazil 2, Italy 1.

Twelve other countries qualified: France, Hungary, Peru, Scotland, Iran, West Germany, Tunisia, Mexico, Austria, Spain, Sweden, Poland.

FONTAINE, Just (France)

Born in Marrakesh, Morocco, in 1933, Fontaine had been struggling to win a permanent place in the French attack during the build-up to the 1958 finals in Sweden. He had been an international player since 1956 but rarely showed his club form at international level. It all came right for him, however, in Sweden when he collected a record 13 goals as he helped power France into a best-ever third place. His haul included four goals in the third-place play-off against West Germany and a hat-trick in his World Cup debut against Paraguay.

He played club football for Nice and Reims and was top League scorer in France in 1958 (34 goals) and in 1960 (28) before a twice-broken leg brought a premature end to his career. He was briefly manager of the French national team and served as President of the Players' Union. Fontaine's prolific partnership with French idol Raymond Kopa was considered one of the most potent pairings in World Cup history.

Dutch striker Johnny Rep outjumps the Argentinian defence in the 1978 World Cup Final to power in a header that struck the bar. Holland came *that* close to winning the match.

FRANCE

Their full record in World Cup tournaments:

1930 Mexico (4–1), Argentina (0–1), Chile (0–1).

1934 Austria (2–3).

1938 Belgium (3–1), Italy (1–3).

1954 Yugoslavia (0–1), Mexico (3–2).

1958 Paraguay (7–3), Yugoslavia (2–3), Scotland (2–1), Northern Ireland (4–0), Brazil (2–5, semi-final), West Germany (6–3). Finished third.

1966 Mexico (1–1), Uruguay (1–2), England (0–2).

1978 Italy (1–2), Argentina (1–2), Hungary (3–1).

Summary: P20 W8 D1 L11 F43 A38

GAETJENS, Larry (USA)

The name Larry Gaetjens is like a knife-thrust in the history of English football. It was his goal that gave the United States a devastating 1–0 victory over England in the 1950 World Cup in Brazil at the Belo Horizonte stadium. Only Italy's defeat by North Korea in the 1966 finals rivals it as a World Cup giant-killing. Gaetjens, a centre-forward who was born in Haiti, scored his stunning goal in the thirty-seventh minute when he deflected a shot from left-half Bahr wide of England's goalkeeper Bert Williams. Some reports described it as an opportunist header; others that the ball had merely struck him and gone into the net.

Efforts to trace Gaetjens for the true story floundered in 1970 when, in his native Haiti, it was reported that he had 'disappeared in mysterious circumstances'. Later unconfirmed reports stated that he had died in a Haitian jail after helping to organise a guerilla movement against the island's dictator, 'Papa' Doc. His name will live on in English football history.

GARRINCHA, Manoel Francisco dos Santos (Brazil)

There has never been another footballer quite like Garrincha, a nickname meaning 'Little Bird'. Born in the mountain village of Pau Grande in 1933, he was a cripple at birth. An operation left one leg shorter than the other and both legs were so bowed you could have run a pig through them without him knowing. But when there was a ball at his feet he could be the most bewitching, bewildering and stunning winger who ever pulled a defence apart. He was such an individualist that even Brazilian coaches, with their preaching of freedom of expression, were petrified of his independent spirit. It was only after a deputation of his team-mates had pleaded on his behalf that he was included in the 1958 World Cup match against Russia.

GARRINCHA . . . an independent spirit.

He and 17-year-old Pele made their World Cup debuts together and they transformed Brazil into an unbeatable side. Garrincha's contribution to the World Cup victories of 1958 and 1962 was greater than anybody's. He tried to motivate the Brazilians again in 1966 but a cartilage operation and injuries collected in a car smash had robbed him of much of his unique magic.

He won 68 caps while playing for Botafogo, Corinthians and Flamengo but his glittering career was tarnished by a series of domestic scandals after he had left his wife and seven daughters to marry a vivacious nightclub singer. There has rarely been anybody to match his skill and invention on a pitch that he always used to turn into a stage.

COMMENTS

'I was in the England World Cup team that Garrincha destroyed with his amazing skill in the 1962 quarter-finals in Chile. The man was a genius. Full stop. He beat our goalkeeper Ron Springett twice, first with a thumping header and then a viciously swerving 20-yard shot that spun into the net like a Jim Laker off-break. When I think of Garrincha I recall a stray dog that invaded the pitch during that quarter-final. It led a posse of players and ballboys a dance before I went down on all fours to capture it. The intruder seemed very relieved when I carried him to the touchline. He rewarded me by sending a yellow stream running down my England shirt and shorts. I ponged so much that at half-time I had to change all my gear. Garrincha, an animal-loving country boy who among other things kept 80 birds in his village home, fell in love with the stray and saw it as a lucky omen that he took command of the game after it had trespassed on to the pitch. He adopted the dog, named it Jimmy Greaves and took it home to Brazil with him!'

GERMANY

(See also East Germany and West Germany.)
Germany competed in two World Cup final tournaments before being split into East and West:

1934 Belgium (5–2), Sweden (2–1), Czechoslovakia (1–3, semi-final), Austria (3–2). Finished third.

1938 Switzerland (1–1, replay 2–4).

GERSON, de Oliveira Nunes (Brazil)

A master strategist, he was the player who plotted Brazil's triumph in the 1970 World Cup. His precise passing from midfield gave Brazil drive and direction and he also packed a powerful finishing shot as he proved with a spectacular goal in the 1970 Final against Italy. Born at Niteroi on the Bay of Rio in 1941, he first came to world prominence in the 1960 Olympic soccer tournament in Italy. He failed to make an impressive impact in his one World Cup appearance in the 1966 finals in England but four years later he emerged as Brazil's key midfield schemer.

Criticised for his lack of enthusiasm in training and for smoking an alleged 40 cigarettes a day, Gerson had a bitter dispute with the manager of the Flamengo club and was transferred to their Rio neighbours Botafogo, for whom his skilled left foot became like a conductor's baton in their race for championship honours. He won 84 caps and wound down his distinguished career with Sao Paulo where a broken ankle forced his retirement in 1973.

GERSON . . . a left foot like a conductor's baton.

GHIGGIA, Alcide (Uruguay)

Nicknamed Chico, Ghiggia was an unlikely looking world-class player. He was 'The Matchstick Man' of Uruguayan football, with spindly legs and a narrow, hunched frame. But his ball control and speed on the right wing demoralised many a full-back and his rocketing right-foot shooting was Uruguay's most devastating weapon in the 1950 finals. He had given notice of his potential a year earlier when, as an amateur, he had starred for Uruguay in the South American championship. He fully lived up to his promise in Rio in the deciding match against Brazil, hammering the goal that clinched a 2–1 victory. Eight years later he played in the World Cup qualifying rounds for Italy and got himself ordered off against Northern Ireland in Belfast.

GOALKEEPERS

Gylmar dos Santos Neves is the only goalkeeper to have collected two World Cup-winners' medals. He was Brazil's last line of defence in 1958 and 1962.

Gordon Banks shares the record for conceding fewest goals for a championship-winning team in a World Cup tournament. He was beaten just three times on the way to England's 1966 triumph, first by a penalty from Eusebio in the semi-final and then by Helmut Haller and Hans Weber in the Final. England played six matches. Enrico Ballesteros (Uruguay, 1930) and Giampiero Combi (Italy, 1934) share the record but played in fewer matches, Ballesteros in four and Combi in five. Jan Jongbloed let in three goals in seven matches for Holland when they finished runners-up in 1974. Emerson Leao conceded three goals in seven matches when Brazil finished third in 1978.

There has been only one instance of a goalkeeper captaining a World Cup-winning team – Combi leading Italy to victory in 1934. Czechoslovakia, their opponents in the Final were skippered by goalkeeper Frantisek Planicka.

Mexican goalkeeper Antonio Carbajal is the only goalkeeper to have played in five World Cup final tournaments (1950/54/58/62/66).

GORDON BANKS . . . beaten only three times in the 1966 Finals.

South Korean Yung Hong Duk holds the back-breaking record of having picked the ball out of the net most times in World Cup final matches. He was beaten 16 times in two matches in the 1954 tournament in Switzerland (0–9 v Hungary and 0–7 v Turkey).

Sepp Maier conceded a goal against Holland in the first minute of the 1974 Final. He then went unbeaten for a record 475 minutes of World Cup final tournament play until Holland scored against West Germany in their fifth match of the 1978 finals.

GOAL SCORERS

The leading scorers in World Cup final tournaments:

Year	Player	Country	Goals	Games
1930	Guillermo Stabile	Argentina	8	4
	Pedro Cea	Uruguay	5	4
	Guillermo Subiabre	Chile	4	3
1934	Angelo Schiavio	Italy	4	4
	Oldrich Nejedly	Czechoslovakia	4	4
	Edmund Conen	Germany	4	4
1938	Leonidas da Silva	Brazil	8	4
	Gyula Szellenger	Hungary	7	4
	Sylvio Piola	Italy	5	4
1950	Ademir	Brazil	7	6
	Juan Schiaffino	Uruguay	5	4
	Basora	Spain	5	6
1954	Sandor Kocsis	Hungary	11	5
	Max Morlock	Germany	6	4
	Erich Probst	Austria	6	5
1958	Just Fontaine	France	13	6
	Helmut Rahn	W. Germany	6	6
	Pele	Brazil	6	4
1962	Florian Albert	Hungary	4	3
	Garrincha	Brazil	4	6
	Valetin Ivanov	Russia	4	4
	Drazen Jerkovic	Yugoslavia	4	6
	Leonel Sanchez	Chile	4	6
	Vava	Brazil	4	6
1966	Eusebio	Portugal	9	6
	Helmut Haller	W. Germany	5	5
	Geoff Hurst	England	4	3
	Franz Beckenbauer	W. Germany	4	6
	Valeriy Porkujan	Russia	4	3
1970	Gerd Muller	W. Germany	10	6
	Jairzinho	Brazil	7	6
	Teofilo Cubillas	Peru	5	4

Year	Player	Country	Goals	Games
1974	Graegorz Lato	Poland	7	7
	Szarmach	Poland	5	5
	Johann Neeskens	Holland	5	7
1978	Mario Kempes	Argentina	6	7
	Robbie Rensenbrink	Holland	5	7
	Teofilo Cubillas	Peru	5	6

Record scores in World Cup final tournaments are: Hungary 9, South Korea 0 (1954); Yugoslavia 9, Zaire 0 (1974). West Germany set the record score for the qualifying rounds in the build-up to the 1970 tournament when they beat Cyprus 12–0 on 21 May 1969. This was beaten by New Zealand in 1981 when they trounced Fiji 13–0 in Auckland.

French inside-left Louis Laurent had the distinction of scoring the first ever World Cup goal in the 4–1 victory over Mexico in the opening match of the 1930 tournament in Uruguay on Sunday, 13 July.

The individual record haul for a World Cup final tournament is the 13 goals Just Fontaine scored for France in 1958. West German striker Gerd Muller notched 10 goals in the 1970 finals and another four in 1974 for a record aggregate of 14. Fontaine and Brazilian right-winger Jairzinho are the only two players to have netted in every match in a final series. Jairzinho collected seven goals in six matches in the 1970 finals in Mexico.

Gerd Muller set an all-time record with 19 goals in 12 matches for West Germany in the 1970 series – nine of them coming in the six qualifying games.

Brazilian striker Vava is the only player to have scored in successive World Cup Finals. He scored two goals against Sweden in the 1958 Final and one against Czechoslovakia in the 1962 Final.

There are two contenders for the title of fastest goal of the World Cup finals: Olle Nyberg, Sweden's outside-left, netted in the first move of the match against Hungary in the 1938 semi-final. Timings for the goal vary from 25 seconds to 35 seconds. Bernard Lacombe's goal for France against Italy in the 1978 tournament was clocked at 31 seconds.

The record score for an individual in one World Cup final match is four goals and is shared by eight players: Gustav Wetterstroem (Sweden v Cuba, 1938); Leonidas da Silva (Brazil v Poland, 1938); Ernest Willimowski (Poland v Brazil, 1938); Ademir (Brazil v Sweden, 1950); Juan Schiaffino (Uruguay v Bolivia, 1950); Sandor Kocsis (Hungary v West Germany, 1954); Just Fontaine (France v West Germany, 1958); Eusebio (Portugal v North Korea, 1966).

GERD MULLER . . . deadly marksman for West Germany.

The most goals in one World Cup finals match came when Austria beat Switzerland 7–5 in a 1954 quarter-final.

Pele and Uwe Seeler set World Cup records within minutes of each other in Mexico on 3 June 1970, when their goals made them the first players to score in four successive World Cup final tournaments.

When Pele scored the first goal against Italy in the 1970 Final it was Brazil's one-hundredth goal in World Cup final tournaments. They have collected a record 119 goals in their 52 World Cup final matches. West Germany are the only other country to have topped 100 goals – 110 in 47 matches, a total that includes the 14 goals credited to Germany in the 1934 and 1938 tournaments.

When Dutchman Robbie Rensenbrink scored from the penalty spot against Scotland in 1978, it was the one-thousandth goal in World Cup finals.

GREN, Gunnar (Sweden)

His two goals helped Sweden win the 1948 Olympic title in London. Ten years later, at the age of 38, he played a prominent part in steering Sweden to the

1958 World Cup Final against Brazil. In between these two triumphs he became one of the world's highest-paid players, starring in the Italian League with AC Milan and later with Florentina and Genoa. Born in Gothenberg in 1920, he was idolised in Milan where he featured in an all-Swedish inside-forward trio with Gunnar Nordhal and Nils Liedholm. He wound down his career in Sweden, continuing to play League Football until the early 1970s. Briefly manager of Juventus, he was known as 'The Professor'.

GROSICS, Gyula (Hungary)

This cool and competent goalkeeper was the magnificent last line of defence for the 'Magical Magyars' for 14 years, winning 89 caps despite a year in the wilderness following a suspension for an alleged smuggling offence. He collected a World Cup runners-up medal in 1954 and also played in the 1958 and 1962 finals. His clubs were Dorog, Honved and Tatabanya.

GYLMAR dos Santos Neves (Brazil)

On 29 June 1969, Gylmar played his one-hundredth and final international match at the back of the Brazilian defence. England, then holders of the World Cup, were the opposition at the Maracana Stadium in Rio. Fittingly for Brazil's greatest goalkeeper, his distinguished international career ended with a 2–1 victory. His first match for Brazil had been back in 1953 and his peak moments came in 1958 and 1962 when he became the only goalkeeper to play for two World Cup-winning teams. He had a long association with Santos after early experience with Jabaquara and then Corinthians. Gylmar was 39 when he bowed out of international football, after conceding just 95 goals in his 100 matches.

HAAN, Arie (Holland)

A powerful and inventive player, Haan collected World Cup runners-up medals with Holland in 1974 and 1978. Though a midfield specialist, he adapted his game to play as a sweeper in defence in 1974 because of a Dutch injury crisis. He was a driving force in the Ajax team that won three successive European Cup Finals and later helped Anderlecht win the European Cup Winners' Cup. Born on 16 November 1948, he got a teachers' diploma before concentrating full-time on football. One of his specialities is a venomous right-foot shot that he used to spectacular effect in the 1978 finals.

HAITI

Haiti have qualified just once for a place in the World Cup finals. They played in West Germany in the 1974 tournament and were right out of their depth after an encouraging start in which they jolted Italy by taking the lead in their group match. Centre-forward Sanon sprinted through the Italian defence to end goalkeeper Dino Zoff's record of not having been beaten for 1,143 minutes. The Italians recovered to win 3–1. Then Haiti were walloped 7–0 by Poland and 4–1 by Argentina.

HALLER, Helmut (West Germany)

Haller was first capped by West Germany at the age of 18 when a virtual 'unknown' with Second Division club Augsburg. Bologna quickly spotted his potential and signed him, a transfer that was delayed while he completed his 1962 World Cup commitments with West Germany. A fast and

HELMUT HALLER . . . theatrical but talented.

aggressive player with good close control, he helped Bologna win the Italian League championship in 1962–64. Two years later he scored one of West Germany's two goals in the 1966 World Cup Final against England.

After a series of disputes with Bologna, he was sold to Juventus in 1968 but he continued to star for West Germany's national team and played a part in their qualification for the 1970 World Cup finals until a damaged shoulder put him out of action. Born near Augsburg in 1939, this blond, stocky forward became equally effective as a midfield schemer.

COMMENTS

'Haller was not the most popular player in the game. He could be a niggling opponent and was infuriating the way he used often to fall about as if shot when tackled. But he was a great competitor and could trouble the tightest defences with his intelligent positioning and accurate shooting ability.'

HERBERGER, Sepp (West Germany)

Born in Mannheim in 1897, this father figure of German football masterminded their game for a quarter of a century. He won three caps while playing for SC Walhorf and VFR Mannheim but it was as a coach that he made his greatest contribution to German football. He was chief coach from the time of the 1938 World Cup finals and handed over to his protégé Helmut Schoen after the 1962 finals

The high point of his career came in 1954 when he steered the unrated West German team to a stunning victory over Hungary in the World Cup Final in Switzerland. Proof of his clever tactical brain came in the early part of the tournament when the Germans played Hungary. Herberger knew he could afford a defeat and still qualify for the Final, so he deliberately fielded a weakened team that was hammered 8–3 by the 'Magical Magyars'. He then put out the strongest team in the Final and Hungary were startled by the power of the opposition and folded to a shock 3–2 defeat.

HIDEGKUTI, Nandor (Hungary)

A right-winger in the Hungarian team that won the 1952 Olympic title, Hidegkuti later developed the deep-lying centre-forward role and it was his hat-trick that inspired the 6–3 downfall of England at

NANDOR HIDEGKUTI . . . a hat-trick against England.

Wembley in 1953. Though more a maker than a taker of goals, Hidegkuti managed to score 39 times in his 68 international appearances. He collected a runners-up medal in the 1954 World Cup and also played against Wales in the 1958 finals in Sweden.

While most of his international team-mates played for the army side Honved, Hidegkuti stayed loyal to MTK Budapest, the club he joined in 1947. Born in Budapest on 3 March 1922, he switched to coaching at the end of his playing career and worked with Fiorentina and Mantova in Italy and then Ujpest Doza and Vasas Gyor at home in Hungary before taking a post in Egypt.

HOENESS, Uli (West Germany)

Hoeness was born in Ulm on 5 January 1952 and started his football career with his local Ulm 46 club. He established himself as a world star while helping Bayern Munich win three successive European Cup finals in the 1970s. Along with a cluster of Bayern clubmates, he became a major influence on the West German team that won the European Nations Cup in 1972 and the World Cup in 1974.

ULI HOENESS... expert at making undetected runs.

At his most effective playing just behind the front line of strikers, he was expert at coming through on undetected runs to collect vital goals, as he proved by scoring twice in Bayern's European Cup Final replay triumph over Atletico Madrid in 1974. He is an intelligent man who would have become an English teacher in Germany had he not made the grade as a footballer. With his close friend Paul Breitner as club skipper, Hoeness started a new career in the 1980s as manager of the Bayern club he served so well as a player.

HOLLAND

Their full record in World Cup final tournaments:

1934 Switzerland (2–3). Eliminated.

1938 Czechoslovakia (0–3). Eliminated.

1974 Uruguay (0–2), Sweden (0–0), Bulgaria (4–1), Argentina (4–0), East Germany (2–0), Brazil (2–0), West Germany (1–2, final). Runners-up.

1978 Iran (3–0), Peru (0–0), Scotland (2–3), Austria (5–1), West Germany (2–2), Italy (2–1), Argentina (1–3, final). Runners-up.

Summary: P16 W8 D3 L5 F32 A19

Holland completed an unhappy record in Buenos Aires in 1978 when they became the first team to finish runners-up in successive Finals. Nine players appeared in both Final matches: Jongbloed, Suurbier, Haan, Krol, Jansen, Neeskens, Rep, Rensenbrink, Rene Van der Kerkhof.

HUNGARY

Their full record in World Cup final tournaments:

1934 Egypt (4–2), Austria (1–2). Eliminated.

1938 Dutch East Indies (6–0), Switzerland (2–0), Sweden (5–1), Italy (2–4, final). Runners-up.

1954 South Korea (9–0), West Germany (8–3), Brazil (4–2), Uruguay (4–2), West Germany (2–3, final). Runners-up.

1958 Wales (1–1), Sweden (1–2), Mexico (4–0), Wales (1–2, play-off).

1962 England (2–1), Bulgaria (6–1), Argentina (0–0), Czechoslovakia (0–1, quarter-finals).

1966 Portugal (1–3), Brazil (3–1), Russia (1–2, quarter-finals).

1978 Argentina (1–2), Italy (1–3), France (1–3).

Summary: P26 W13 D2 L11 F73 A42

When the Hungarians arrived in Switzerland for the 1954 tournament, they were the hottest favourites of all time. They had gone four years without a single defeat, had won the 1952 Olympic title and had smashed 13 goals into the England net in two matches. Their unbeaten record finally crashed at the heartbreak hurdle of the 1954 Final. A gamble of playing field marshal Ferenc Puskas when half-fit had blown up in their faces and unheralded West Germany became the new champions. But that Hungarian team of the early 1950s will always be remembered as one of the greatest combinations ever to operate on a football pitch.

HUNT, Roger (England)

Hunt scored 18 goals in 34 international matches for England, none more vital than the three he collected in the eliminating series of the 1966 finals (two against France and one against Mexico). Born in Golborne, Lancashire, on 20 July 1938, this big-hearted striker will always be associated with Liverpool for whom he scored a club record 254 League goals between 1959 and 1969. He wound down his distinguished career with Bolton Wanderers before retiring in 1972 to concentrate on his family road haulage business.

ROGER HUNT . . . a player's player.

COMMENTS

'England have not had a more industrious and determined player in their attack than Roger who was always prepared to run himself into the ground for the team cause. His control and finishing accuracy in restricted penalty area space meant he could also be a devastating individual player. But it was his selfless running off the ball that made him such an invaluable member of the 1966 World Cup-winning team. Roger and I were friends as well as rivals and there was never any friction between us when one was left out at the expense of the other. He was a good sportsman as well as a players' player.'

HURST, Geoff (England)

The name Geoff Hurst was cemented into World Cup history the day he scored the glorious hat-trick that won the Jules Rimet trophy for England at Wembley in 1966. He also scored the crucial winning goal against Argentina in the quarter-finals when he came into the attack for his World Cup debut.

The son of a professional footballer, Hurst was born at Ashton-under-Lyme, Lancashire, on 8 December 1941. He netted 180 League goals for West Ham and 22 for Stoke before playing briefly for West Brom. Hurst then became player-manager of Telford United, a stepping stone to a job as manager of Chelsea with whom he had a brief, eventful association. He is an important member of Ron Greenwood's England training team.

COMMENTS

'Geoff took my place in the England attack in the 1966 World Cup quarter-finals after I had been injured. The media drummed up a lot of controversy when Geoff kept his place for the Final at my expense. He ended all arguments with his magnificent hat-trick. There have been few more effective strikers in an England shirt than Geoff at his peak and his understanding with clubmates Bobby Moore and Martin Peters meant he slotted smoothly into the scheme of things. He was always positive, both in his attitude and his action, and his honest endeavour made him a great example for young players. What can I say but Hurst, Hurst Hurst . . . !'

GEOFF HURST . . . 'always positive in his attitude and his action.'

IRAN

Iran have made one appearance in the World Cup finals and marked the achievement by a surprise draw with Scotland. They qualified for the 1978 tournament in Argentina and on paper looked certain to be outgunned in a group that also included Holland and Peru. They went down 0–3 to the Dutch and were beaten 4–1 by Peru but sandwiched in between was a 1–1 draw that stunned Scotland. What made it particularly embarrassing for the Scots is that they were only saved from defeat by an own goal.

ISRAEL

Israel qualified for the World Cup finals in 1970 and equipped themselves well in their three matches: Uruguay (0–2), Sweden (1–1) and Italy (0–0). Their most impressive player was Mordecai Spiegler, a scheming-scoring inside-left who was born in Russia. Ron Greenwood, then manager of West Ham, was so impressed that he invited Spiegler to join West Ham but there were problems over his registration. Israel thought they had qualified for the 1958 finals after the withdrawal of all their opponents from the qualification group for political reasons. But FIFA ordered them to play Wales, who had been eliminated by Czechoslovakia, and the Welsh team won 2–0 home and away to earn the trip to Sweden.

ITALY

Their full record in World Cup final tournaments:

1934 USA (7–1), Spain (1–1, replay 1–0), Austria (1–0), Czechoslovakia (2–1, final). Champions.

1938 Norway (2–1), France (3–1), Brazil (2–1), Hungary (4–2, final). Champions.

1950 Sweden (2–3), Paraguay (2–0).

1954 Switzerland (1–2), Belgium (4–1), Switzerland (1–4, play-off).

1962 West Germany (0–0), Chile (0–2), Switzerland (3–0).

1966 Chile (2–0), Russia (0–1), North Korea (0–1).

1970 Sweden (1–0), Uruguay (0–0), Israel (0–0), Mexico (4–1), West Germany (4–3), Brazil (1–4, final). Runners-up.

Italy surprisingly failed to reach the quarter-finals in the 1954 tournament despite the powerful presence of Inter-Milan striker Benito 'Poison' Lorenzi, pictured unleashing a shot against Switzerland.

1974 Haiti (3–1), Argentina (1–1), Poland (1–2).

1978 France (2–1), Hungary (3–1), Argentina (1–0), West Germany (0–0), Austria (1–0), Holland (1–2), Brazil (1–2). Finished fourth.

Summary: P36 W20 D6 L10 A40

Italy share with Brazil (3), Uruguay (2) and West Germany (2) the honour of having won the World Cup more than once. Their performance in 1970 when they finished runners-up to Brazil helped wipe out the memory of their nightmare in the 1966 finals in England. After an unbelievable 1–0 defeat by North Korea, the Italian team were pelted with eggs and tomatoes by a crowd of protesting fans on their arrival home in Italy. Giacinto Facchetti, Italian skipper in 1970 and a survivor of the 1966 disaster against the Koreans, said 'The terrible reception we received on our return home was the biggest motivating factor for us four years later in Mexico. We knew we just daren't let ourselves or our supporters down in Mexico'.

JAIR, Rosta Pinto (Brazil)

This immensely skilled inside-forward came close to steering Brazil to a World Cup triumph in the 1950 finals. In the deciding match against Uruguay, he was the one player who was a constant threat to the defence-dominated Uruguayan team. He was a subtle positional player and a master of the swerved shot and penetrative passing. It was his inventive touches that made him such a vital member of the famous Brazilian inside-forward trio along with Zizinho and Ademir.

Born in Barra Mansa, Rio, in 1921, he spent the early part of his careeer with Vasco da Gama and Madureira before joining Flamengo and then Fluminense. He won 39 caps with Brazil and was one of their biggest heroes in the immediate post-war years. (He is not to be confused with Jair da Costa, a Brazilian winger who was understudy to Garrincha before making an impressive impact in Europe with Inter Milan in the 1960s.)

JAIRZINHO, Jair Ventura Filho (Brazil)

Jairzinho rivals even the legendary Garrincha for the title of Brazil's most dynamic and exciting winger. In the 1970 World Cup he became the first player to score in every game including the Final. He pre-

JAIRZINHO . . . disturbing the Italian defence in the 1970 World Cup Final in Mexico City.

ferred to play down the middle in his formative years but it was when he took over from the injured Garrincha on the right wing for Botafogo in 1963 that Brazil realised they had unearthed yet another world-class star.

Jairzinho, born in 1944, showed he had courage and character to go with his skill when he battled his way back into the Brazilian team after a leg operation that threatened to end his career in 1967. He was a jet-paced player who could finish runs with a deadly accurate right-foot cross-shot. He played in three World Cup finals (1966/70/74) and in 1981 he returned to Botafogo after a globe-trotting period that saw him playing for clubs in France, Venezuela and Bolivia.

JONGBLOED, Jan (Holland)

Holland took 34-year-old FC Amsterdam veteran Jan Jongbloed to the 1974 World Cup finals in West Germany as third-choice goalkeeper. But suddenly he was thrust into the team following injuries to the two men ahead of him. He was one of the revelations of the tournament, his adventurous and often spectacular goalkeeping continually coming to Holland's rescue as they produced the cavalier charges that took them to runners-up position

Jongbloed was summoned for World Cup duty again four years later and there was furious dissent in the Dutch camp when he was dropped after the match against Scotland. Mrs Jongbloed stepped forward as a spokesperson for her husband and made no secret of what she thought of manager Ernst Happel's decison. Piet Schrijvers, his replacement, was injured against Italy and Jongbloed was recalled to help Holland become the runners-up for the second successive time. Following FC Amsterdam's relegation, he signed for Roda JC and proved that, at 38, he was still a reliable last line of defence by keeping a blank sheet in his first five games.

KEMPES, Mario (Argentina)

Kempes turned the 1978 World Cup into a showcase for his glittering talent, scoring most goals in the tournament (six in seven games) and doing more than anybody to capture the world championship for Argentina. Born in Cordoba in 1955, he played in the 1974 World Cup finals as a 19-year-old striker but was overshadowed by players like Rene Houseman, Carlos Babington and Miguel Brindisi. His game flourished after he had left his local club Rosario Central and joined Valencia in Spain in 1976. He was top scorer for Valencia in his first two seasons and the Spanish club were so pleased with his form that they signed him to a new five-year contract before he returned to Argentina for the 1978 World Cup.

MARIO KEMPES . . . turned the 1978 World Cup into a showcase for his talent.

He looked a £3-million player in the finals, continually taking the eye with his speed of thought and action, his superb balance and deadly accurate finishing. He was equally effective in midfield or in any front-line position and was particularly devastating when in harness with Leopold Luque. Fittingly, it was his two goals that clinched the 3–1 victory over Holland in the Final. It was possibly the peak performance of his career because there was a definite slackening of his output on his return to Valencia and in 1981 he went home to Argentina to join River Plate, where he linked up with six of his World Cup colleagues – goalkeeper Fillol, defenders Passarella and Tarantini, midfielder Alonso and wingers Ortiz and Houseman.

KOCSIS, Sandor (Hungary)

Kocsis was such a formidable force in the air that he was nicknamed 'Golden Head'. The leading marksman in the 1954 World Cup tournament with 11 goals, he clinched a place for Hungary in the Final with two headed goals in extra-time of a classic semi-final against Uruguay. An indication of his goal-scoring powers is that he netted seven hat-tricks for Hungary in a total of 75 goals.

He was leading Hungarian League scorer with Honved in 1951 (30 goals), 1952 (36) and 1954 (33). Born in 1929, he joined his favourite club Ferencvaros in 1942 but was later co-opted by the army club Honved. Following the 1956 Hungarian Uprising, he signed for Barcelona along with countryman Zoltan Czibor.

KOPA, Raymond (France)

Playing as a creative, deep-lying centre-forward, Raymond Kopa was the engineer and Just Fontaine the executioner for the French team that swept to third place in the 1958 World Cup finals. The son of a French mother and a Polish father called Kopaczewski, Kopa was born at Noeux-les-Mines in 1931 and won the first of his 45 international caps in 1952

He was a crowd-pulling star with Angers, Reims and Real Madrid and played in four successive European Cup Finals for two different clubs (first with Reims against Real Madrid in 1956 and then the next three with Real). Kopa was never totally settled in Madrid where he had to play second fiddle to the great Di Stefano. He wound down his career back at Reims and again in partnership with Just Fontaine.

KROL, Rudi (Holland)

This versatile defender – equally efficient as an attacking full-back or as an adventurous sweeper – skippered the Dutch team that finished runners-up in the 1978 World Cup and was a key member of the 1974 team in West Germany. Born on 24 March 1949, he started his club career with Rood Wit and established himself as a world star after joining Ajax in 1968. A broken leg stopped him playing in the 1971 European Cup Final but he helped Ajax win the trophy in the following two seasons.

The most capped of all Dutch internationals with more than 75 appearances to his credit, he had a spell in the United States with Vancouver White Caps before joining Napoli in Italy. He is a linguist who has mastered German, English and Italian and is always articulate with his flowing football.

LATO, Grzegorz (Poland)

He signalled his arrival as a world-class player with his superb performances for Poland in the 1974 World Cup qualifying matches when England were among the teams 'Pole-axed'. Born on 8 April 1950, he helped Stal Mielic win the Polish League championship before joining the international team for the World Cup finals in West Germany. The Poles had lost their star forward Wlodzimierz Lubanski with injury but Lato compensated for his absence by growing in stature and his strong right-foot shooting brought him the tournament's top haul of seven goals, the last of which earned Poland third place. He was prominent again for Poland in the 1978 finals but this time more as a goal-maker than a goal-taker. Though scoring only two goals in six matches, he troubled every defence he faced with his acceleration and deft touches.

LEONIDAS, da Silva (Brazil)

Known as 'The Black Diamond' of Brazilian football, this stocky centre-forward was an acrobatic player who specialised in overhead 'bicycle' kicks and had a full repertoire of ball tricks with which to baffle and bewilder defences. He was top scorer in the 1938 World Cup finals with eight goals, including a first-half hat-trick against Poland. He made it four goals in extra-time to lift Brazil to a dramatic 6–5 victory.

Born in 1913, Leonidas was a much-travelled player who featured with a cluster of clubs in a spectacular 19-year career – Havanesa, Barroso, Sun Americano, Sirio Libanes, Bomsucesso, Nacional, Vasco da Gama, Botafogo, Flamengo and Sao Paulo. He was capped 23 times. He later became a radio reporter and then a private detective.

LIEDHOLM, Nils (Sweden)

Liedholm's immaculate ball control and intelligent positional sense made him the 'Master' of Swedish football and he steered IFK Norrkoping to five League championship triumphs in the 1950s. He came to international prominence when his precise passes helped Sweden win the Olympic title in London in 1948. A year later and his Swedish team-mates Gunnar Nordhal and Gunnar Gren followed Norrkoping manager Lajos Czeizler to AC Milan and they became the most feared inside-forward trio in the Italian League.

The peak performances of his career came in the 1958 World Cup when he captained the Swedish team into runners-up position. He gave the Final against Brazil a spectacular send-off with a magni-

ficent goal. After winning four championship medals with Milan, he became their coach and then manager. He has more recently coached Naples and AS Roma. Born on 8 October 1922, he played until he was 40.

LUQUE, Leopoldo (Argentina)

He played an important part in Argentina's 1978 World Cup triumph as plundering partner to Mario Kempes. Luque lacked the finesse and flair of Kempes but his expert laying-off of the ball and his strength in the penalty area made the going easier for his talented team-mate. He also has a powerful right-foot shot that troubled every goalkeeper he faced. The goal he scored from outside the box against France was one of the most spectacular of the finals. He recovered from a shoulder injury and the nightmare of having his brother killed in a car crash during the tournament to help prompt Kempes to his match-winning performance in the Final. Luque was with River Plate in 1978 but later rejoined Union, his original club, before taking his talent into the Mexican league with Tampica.

GRZEGORZ LATO . . . a powerhouse player for Poland.

MAIER, Sepp (West Germany)

Sepp Maier, with a distinctive style and appearance, became one of the world's most renowned goalkeepers. His consistency, both for West Germany and Bayern Munich, was almost uncanny. He did not miss a single club game between 20 August 1966 and the end of the 1978–79 season. That was a run of 442 games, during which six understudies came and went without getting a single first-team game. His remarkable run was ended by a car crash at the start of the 1979–80 season.

He was a safe and reliable last line of defence for the Bayern team that monopolised the European Cup for three years from 1974 to 1976. He played in five World Cup matches for West Germany in 1970 and collected a winners' medal in 1974. Maier set a record of being unbeaten for 475 minutes in World Cup finals from the moment of Johann Neeskens' first-minute penalty for Holland in the 1974 Final to Arie Haan's long-range shot for the Dutchmen in West Germany's fifth game of the 1978 finals.

SEPP MAIER . . . distinctive in style and appearance.

MANAGERS

The managers of the World Cup winning teams:

1930 Odino Viera (Uruguay).
1934/1938 Vittorio Pozzo (Italy).
1950 Colonel Volpe (Uruguay).
1954 Sepp Herberger (West Germany).
1958 Vicente Feola (Brazil).
1962 Aymore Moreira (Brazil).
1966 Sir Alf Ramsey (England).
1970 Mario Zagola (Brazil).
1974 Helmut Schoen (West Germany).
1976 Cesar Luis Menotti (Argentina).

MASPOLI, Roque (Uruguay)

The last line of defence for the Uruguayan team that won the World Cup in 1950, Maspoli was rated one of the greatest of all South American goalkeepers. He played in three matches in 1950 and was back in World Cup action again four years later when his safe hands helped push Uruguay into the semi-final, where they were beaten in extra-time in a classic confrontation with Hungary. At the end of his distinguished career he became a top-ranking coach and eventually manager of Penarol, the club with whom he established himself as a world star. While manager of Penarol he helped develop the talents of Ladislao Mazurkiewicz, the one player who can challenge Maspoli as the finest goalkeeper in Uruguayan football history.

MATTHEWS, Sir Stanley (England)

The shuffling 'Wizard of Dribble' played in two World Cup final tournaments during his remarkable 33-year career. He was a member of the England squad in 1950 but was not called into action until after the sensational 1–0 defeat by the United States. He played just the one game, England going down 1–0 to Spain and getting eliminated. Four years later he played two matches in the 1954 tournament at the age of 39. In 1956 he became the first player to be voted European Footballer of the Year but the

STANLEY MATTHEWS . . . the shuffling 'Wizard of Dribble.' ▶

selectors surprisingly left him out of England's squad for the 1958 World Cup finals.

Born at Hanley on 1 February 1915, Stanley Matthews became in 1965 the first player knighted for his services to the game. He played his first match for Stoke City at the age of 17 and his final game for them at 50. In between he had 14 spectacularly productive years with Blackpool. He won 54 caps, not counting 29 wartime international appearances.

COMMENTS

'I couldn't for the life of me understand why the selectors left Stanley Matthews out of the 1958 World Cup squad. I was a young pro in the game with Chelsea at the time and the consensus of opinion was that even at 43 he was still the king. He was *the* most famous footballer in the world and even if just from a psychological point of view it would have been worth having him in Sweden where full-backs would have been petrified of him because of his reputation. He was far from over the hill as he proved five years later by inspiring Stoke's promotion charge to the First Division and winning the Footballer of the Year award for a second time.'

MAURO, Ramos de Oliveira (Brazil)

Capped for the first time by Brazil in 1949, Mauro took nearly 12 years to establish himself as their Number One centre-half. He was called up so many times for standby duty in the Brazilian squad that he became known as 'the eternal substitute'. But his patience was rewarded when he was elected captain of the 1962 World Cup squad and it was he who collected the Jules Rimet Trophy after Brazil had beaten Czechoslovakia in the Final.

Born in 1930, Mauro was discovered by Sao Paulo while playing in the middle of the Sao Joao defence in 1948. He was selected for his first cap after starring for Sao Paolo in a victory over a touring Arsenal team, then considered the greatest club in world football.

COMMENTS

'Mauro impressed during the 1962 finals with his positional play and his coolness and composure under pressure. There were strong rumours before the tournament started that Bellini, the centre-half who had led Brazil to their 1958 triumph, was going to be recalled but they stuck by Mauro and he justified his place with a series of sound performances.'

MAZZOLA, Sandrino (Italy)

Italian idol Valentino Mazzola, captain of the national side and League champions Torino, left two sons to carry on the Mazzola football legend when he died in the air disaster that killed the entire Torino team in 1949. The two Mazzola boys, Sandrino and Feruccio, both became top-quality professional players. It was Sandrino who flourished his great scheming skill on the World Cup stage. He marked his World Cup debut against Chile in England in 1966 with a goal that helped lift Italy to a 2–0 victory and it was his measured passes that guided the Italians into the 1970 Final against Brazil.

Born in Turin on 8 November 1942, Sandrino started his career as a striker for Inter-Milan but later developed into a magnificent midfield marshal whose linking work was preferred to that of 'Golden Boy' Gianni Rivera in the 1970 tournament. Following his retirement he became an executive director of Inter.

MEAZZA, Guiseppe (Italy)

Guiseppe Meazza, nicknamed Peppino, was a slim and elegant player who was quick and dangerous in any of the three inside-forward positions. He collected a winners' medal with Italy in 1934 and four years later captained the team that retained the World Cup with a 4–2 victory over Hungary in the Final in Paris.

Born in Milan on 23 August 1910, Meazza was happiest at centre-forward but played as an inside-right in both World Cup tournaments. He scored 33 goals in 53 international appearances and another 322 in club football. His peak years were with Inter-Milan with whom he started and finished his career, playing in between for AC Milan, Juventus, Varese and Atlanta. He later had a spell as Inter manager before concentrating on youth-team coaching.

SANDRO MAZZOLA . . . followed in father's footsteps.

CESAR LUIS MENOTTI . . . hailed as a hero in Argentina.

MENOTTI, Cesar Luis (Argentina)

Cesar Luis Menotti was 36 when he was appointed manager of Argentina late in 1974 and he was quickly nicknamed *'El Loco'* – 'The Madman' – when he talked of trying to capture the World Cup with an attacking style of football. It meant altering radically the defensive pattern of play that had plagued the Argentinian game. Just short of four years later Menotti was hailed as a hero when the Argentinian team provided action to go with his words, winning the World Cup with an exciting and adventurous brand of football in which skill and flair rose above the cynical play that had so often scarred their reputation in the past.

Born in Rosario in 1939, Menotti started his playing career with local First Division club Rosario Central. He caused a sensation in 1967 when he defected to the North American Soccer League with the now disbanded New York Generals. His coach was former Birmingham City manager Freddie Goodwin and he teamed up in attack with English centre-forward George Kirby. The slim, long-faced Menotti should have carried a government health warning during the 1978 World Cup when he chain-smoked his way through a pack of cigarettes each time Argentina played.

MEXICO

Their full record in World Cup final tournaments:

1930 France (1–4), Chile (0–3), Argentina (3–6).

1950 Brazil (0–4), Yugoslavia (1–4), Switzerland (1–2).

1954 Brazil (0–5), France (2–3).

1958 Sweden (0–3), Wales (1–1), Hungary (0–4).

1962 Brazil (0–2), Spain (0–1), Czechoslovakia (3–1).

1966 France (1–1), England (0–2), Uruguay (0–0).

1970 Russia (0–0), El Salvador (4–0), Belgium (1–0), Italy (1–4, quarter-finals).

1978 Tunisia (1–3), West Germany (0–6), Poland (1–3).

Summary: P24 W3 D4 L17 F21 A62

Mexico reluctantly hold the record of having had most defeats in World Cup finals (17) and have also conceded most goals (62).

MONTI, Luisito (Argentina and Italy)

A tough and ruthless competitor, Monti became a footballing hero in two countries during a long and eventful career. He was born in Buenos Aires in 1901 to parents with strong Italian roots. Monti played as an attacking centre-half in the Argentinian team beaten by Uruguay in the 1928 Olympics Final and then in the 1930 World Cup Final.

He was 30 and had appeared in 17 internationals with Argentina when Juventus signed him from Boca Juniors. Because of his Italian ancestry, he was eligible to play for Italy and was influential as a schemer based in the middle of the defence when they won the World Cup in 1934. Known in Italy as 'The Man Who Strolls', Monti helped Juventus win four successive League championships. He was a viciously hard but skilful player who collected 18 Italian caps.

MOORE, Bobby (England)

Bobby Moore completed a unique hat-trick when he climbed the Wembley steps as England captain in 1966 to collect the World Cup after the dramatic 4–2 extra-time victory over West Germany. He had made the same triumphant ascent at Wembley in the previous two years as West Ham skipper, first to lift the FA Cup in 1964 and 12 months later to pick up the European Cup Winners' Cup.

Moore shares with Bobby Charlton the record of playing most World Cup finals matches for England. They appeared in 14 games together in the campaigns of 1962, 1966 and 1970. He has a record England caps' collection of 108, and was voted Player of the Tournament in 1966 and was again England's outstanding performer in Mexico in 1970.

COMMENTS

'England have not had a finer servant than Bobby Moore. He was an immaculate defender, stamping his authority on every match that he graced with his presence. Bobby "read" the game better than anybody I ever played with or against and was a master at positioning and of turning defence into attack with intelligently placed passes. He always played with great dignity, never more so than in the 1970 World Cup when lesser players would have crumbled under the pressure put on him just before the finals by a trumped-up jewellery theft charge in Bogota. Bobby can be bracketed with Bobby Charlton and Stanley Matthews as England's greatest football ambassador.'

MOREIRA, Aimore (Brazil)

This renowned coach and his brother Zeze completed a unique family double in the World Cup. Zeze was manager of the Brazilian team in the 1954 tournament and Aimore was in charge when Brazil retained the World Cup in Chile in 1962. Aimore had been an excellent goalkeeper with Botafogo in Rio and, later, Palmeiras in Sao Paulo, and was Brazil's last line of defence for two years in the early 1940s. He had his first chance as Brazil's coach in 1953 but was dismissed following a shock defeat by Paraguay in the South American championships in Peru. Zeze took over but was replaced by Vicente Feola for the 1958 World Cup. Aimore got his chance when Feola became ill during the build-up to the 1962 finals in Chile.

MOROCCO

Morocco's qualification for the 1970 finals made them the first African nation to appear in the decisive stages of the World Cup since Egypt had been beaten by Hungary at Naples in 1934. They shocked West Germany by taking an early lead in their first match and were unlucky to go down 2–1. Then they held the adventurous Peruvians to 0–0 for

BOBBY MOORE and PELE after Brazil had beaten England 1–0 in the 1970 World Cup finals. A Master acknowledging a Master. ▶

66 minutes befor caving in to a 3–0 defeat. In their final match they held Bulgaria to a 1–1 draw and left behind them an impression that African football was clearly alive, well and kicking! They were well prepared by former Yugoslav international goalkeeper Vidinic who four years later performed another minor miracle by guiding Zaire to the finals.

MULLER, Gerd (West Germany)

Nicknamed '*Der Bomber*', Muller blitzed defences with more explosive results than any other striker in World Cup history. Including qualifying matches, Muller scored 19 goals in the 1970 series with 10 in the finals. His contribution to West Germany's World Cup triumph in 1974 was four goals and he had a record finals aggregate of 14. He was just as prolific in club football with Bayern Munich, for whom he scored more than 600 goals in all competitions.

Born in Bavaria on 3 November 1945, he started his career with his local club TSV Nordlingen and joined Bayern in 1964 after several clubs had decided he was too thick-set and stocky to be sufficiently mobile against top defences. His 36 goals in European Cup football made nonsense of that opinion. He had scored 68 goals in 62 matches for West Germany when he announced his retirement from international football before exporting his goal power to the United States.

COMMENTS

'Muller's goal-scoring record says everything that needs to be said. He was a master of the penalty area, continually a thought and a deed ahead of defenders. His finishing was deadly and he had courage to go with his great competitive spirit. For somebody so stocky and heavily built, he could really climb for vital headers and his shooting was equally powerful from either foot. He made the hardest job of all – scoring goals – look easy.'

NASAZZI, Jose (Uruguay)

Like Bobby Moore in 1966, Nasazzi completed a unique hat-trick when he became the first captain to collect the Jules Rimet Trophy after Uruguay's victory over Argentina in the 1930 Final. In 1924 and again in 1928 Nasazzi had led Uruguay to the Olympic championship, which was then considered the world crown of football. Nasazzi was a full-back but, playing the South American way, he patrolled mainly in the middle of the defence. He was noted for the strength and swiftness of his tackle and for the way he always *played* rather than blasted the ball out of defence. His remarkable record as Uruguay captain stretched from 1919 until 1930 and included six South American championship successes as well as the two Olympic titles and the World Cup triumph. He also helped Nacional of Montevideo win seven Uruguayan League titles.

NEESKENS, Johan (Holland)

The driving force of the great Ajax and Dutch international teams, Neeskens provided the midfield motivation that married perfectly with the marvellous skill and flair of Johan Cruyff. Born on 15 September 1951, he was an outstanding all-rounder at school who shone at football, baseball and basketball. But it was football that became his Number One sport and he was quickly established as a star player with Ajax after starting his career with Haarlem. He later took his talent to Barcelona and then New York Cosmos. A key man in the Dutch teams that twice finished runners-up in World Cup Finals, he scored Holland's dramatic first-minute penalty against West Germany in the 1974 Final.

NETTO, Igor (Russia)

Captain of the Russian team that reached the 1962 World Cup quarter-finals, Netto was an inspiring half-back who later in his distinguished career switched successfully to a centre-back role. Born in 1930, he played for Moscow Spartak for 14 seasons and was a powerful influence on the team that won the Russian League title five times and the cup three times. He skippered the Russian side that won the 1956 Olympic title but injury restricted his 1958 World Cup contribution to just one appearance. Capped 56 times, he was awarded Russia's highest honour, the Order of Lenin, and later worked with the sports department of Moscow Radio and became a respected coach. The highlight of his playing career came in 1960 when he led Russia to victory in the first European Nations Cup tournament.

NORTH KOREA

No country has caused a bigger sensation in one World Cup finals appearance than North Korea. They started nervously in the 1966 tournament against Russia, losing 3–0. But a 1–1 draw with Bulgaria improved their confidence and they then shocked group favourites Italy by winning 1–0 to qualify for the quarter-finals against Portugal. The tiny Koreans, few of them more than 5ft 5in. tall, rushed into a 3–0 lead over Portugal and, astonishingly, looked set for a place in the semi-final. Then Eusebio took over and in a spectacular one-man revival movement scored four goals and made another as he lifted Portugal to a dramatic 5–3 victory. The brave and enthusiastic North Koreans had given Asia its finest hour in World Cup history.

NORTHERN IRELAND

Inspired by the persuasive tongue of team manager Peter Doherty and the organisational genius of skipper Danny Blanchflower, Northern Ireland qualified for the 1958 World Cup with football that

JOHAN NEESKENS . . . celebrating the creation of a goal against Italy in the 1978 World Cup finals.

JIMMY McILROY . . . a pass master for Northern Ireland.

was simple yet stunningly effective. They reached the finals in Sweden at the expense of group favourites Italy. They should have played their decisive qualifying match against Italy in Belfast in December 1957 but FIFA-appointed referee Istvan Zsolt of Hungary was held up by fog. The Italians refused to accept an Irish referee and the two teams played a charade of a match that was labelled a friendly but was overloaded with ill-feeling. The game ended in a bad-tempered 2–2 draw. The following month they met again, this time for real and a flood of flowing football by the Irish was rewarded with a 2–1 victory.

In the finals, they played with flair and fire and beat Czechoslovakia 2–1 in a group play-off to clinch a place against France in the quarter-finals, where they were sunk 4–0 by the opportunitism of two-goal Fontaine and the cunning of Kopa. In their group matches they beat Czechoslovakia 1–0, were beaten 1–3 by Argentina and held West Germany to a 2–2 draw.

A feature of Northern Ireland's performances was the mastery in midfield of Blanchflower and the elegant Jimmy McIlroy. Few teams in the competition could match their creative force. The Northern Ireland team that played in the quarter-finals was: Gregg, Keith, McMichael, Blanchflower, Cunningham, Cush, Bingham, Casey, Scott, McIlroy, McParland.

NORWAY

The highlight of Norway's World Cup history was their startling 2–1 victory over England in a qualifying match for the 1982 finals. In the 1938 tournament they performed with credit in the only match they have played in the World Cup finals, when Italy, the defending and eventual champions, had to go to extra-time before eliminating them. Norway had fielded virtually the same team that had collected a bronze medal in the 1936 Berlin Olympics.

NOVAK, Ladislav (Czechoslovakia)

This accomplished left-back for Czechoslovakia in three World Cup final tournaments touched a marvellous peak in 1962 when he was captain of the Czech team that finished runners-up to Brazil. Novak, an alert and often adventurous defender, was capped a record 75 times and played with distinction for Dukla Prague before winding down his career as player-coach with Jablonec. Born in Louny in 1931, Novak won eight championship medals with Dukla after first establishing himself in the Tatran Teplice defence. He had a short spell in charge of the Czech national team.

OCWIRK, Ernst (Austria)

Known as 'Clockwork Ocwirk' because of the precise timing of his passes and runs, and for the fact that he made the teams he played for tick with his intelligent positioning and polished ball control, Ocwirk was the last of the great roaming centre-halves before their duties became almost totally defensive. Born in Vienna in 1926, he played for Stalau and FAC Vienna before joining FK Austria for the peak years of his career. In 1956 he moved to Sampdoria of Genoa and for five years became an idol in the Italian League with his subtle midfield scheming.

He won 62 caps with Austria and scored two goals while helping to steer the Austrians into third place in the 1954 World Cup finals. His first goal came during the astonishing quarter-finals, in which Austria beat Switzerland 7–5, and his second was scored against Uruguay in the match to decide third place. He wound down his playing career with FK Austria before taking over as manager, and later became a travelling coach with assignments in Italy, West Germany and Austria. Included in his many representative appearances were two games for the Rest of Europe against Britain, at Wembley in 1953 and then in Belfast in 1955 when he was the team captain.

ODDITIES

There have been some strange happenings on and off the pitch in World Cup final tournaments as this collection of oddities will reveal:

- The United States trainer raced on to the pitch to protest to the referee over a disputed decision during the 1930 semi-final against Argentina. He stumbled and dropped his box of medical supplies and a bottle of chloroform smashed on the pitch. The trainer took the fumes full in the face as he bent to pick up the box. He folded slowly to the ground like a puppet that has had its strings cut away and had to be carried back to the touchline bench!

- Uruguay and Argentina both insisted on using a 'home' manufactured ball in the first World Cup Final in 1930. Belgian referee John Langenus, resplendent in knickerbockers and a natty striped tie, came out for the kick-off with a ball under each arm, one made in Uruguay and the other in Argentina. The two captains tossed, Manuel Ferreira winning the right for Argentina to use *their* ball for the first 45 minutes. Uruguay, 2–1 down at half-time, used *their* ball in the second-half and won the match 4–2.

• 'By Royal Appointment' took on a new meaning when Romania entered the first World Cup tournament in Uruguay in 1930. King Carol II insisted that a representative team be sent, after the invitation to play had at first been turned down because the players could not get the necessary three months off work. The King selected the team himself and then arranged time off for each of the players with full pay. They were eliminated from the tournament after playing just two matches. When King Carol was overthrown in 1940, he fled to South America where he was warmly remembered as the 'football-mad' king.

• Hector Castro, scorer of Uruguay's victory-clinching fourth goal in the 1930 Final, had only one hand. He had lost his right hand and part of his arm in a childhood accident.

• Ten chartered boats spilling over with Argentinian supporters sailed across the River Plate to Montevideo. Only the first two to sail docked in time for the 1930 Final. The other eight were delayed by thick fog. Match referee John Langenus was aboard the first of the boats.

• There was bitter disappointment in Buenos Aires in 1930 when the news of Argentina's defeat by Uruguay was relayed back from Montevideo. Police opened fire to disperse an angry mob who were attacking the Uruguayan Consulate with bricks and stones. Several days later there was open revolution on the streets of Buenos Aires and the country's President Irigoyen was overthrown in a military coup. It was accepted that the deep disappointment over the World Cup defeat had helped fan the flames of revolution.

• In Montevideo the triumphant Uruguayan players, alleged amateurs, were feted and paraded as national heroes. The municipality of Montevideo decided to reward them by presenting each player with a plot of land that included a newly built house.

• Captain Alex Villaplane proudly led France out against Mexico for the first ever World Cup match on Sunday afternoon, 13 July 1930, the day before Bastille Day. Fifteen years later the same Alex Villaplane was shot by French resistance fighters for allegedly collaborating with the Nazis during the Second World War.

• Swiss centre-forward Poldi Kielholz, scorer of three goals in the 1934 finals tournament, wore spectacles.

• Allemandi, left-back in the Italian team that won the World Cup in 1934, was once banned from football 'for life' after being found guilty of accepting a bribe. He was alleged to have accepted a 50,000-lire payment from a Torino director to give less than his best for Juventus against Torino. Allemandi was later reinstated and was at one time captain of the national team.

• Argentinian-born Raimondo Orsi scored a spectacular goal for Italy against Czechoslovakia in the 1934 Final, his right-foot shot sending the ball on a curling trail into the net. The day after the Final Orsi tried more than 20 times to repeat the shot for the benefit of a posse of photographers. He failed each time.

• Leonidas da Silva, flamboyant star of Brazil's 1938 attack, was unhappy playing against Poland on the muddy pitch at Strasbourg. He decided he would have better footing if he went back to his boyhood days and played barefooted. But the moment he removed his boots and tossed them nonchalantly over the touchline, the referee ordered him to put them back on because it was in contravention of the laws of the game to play without boots. The game was held up while Leonidas replaced his boots and he was sure-footed enough to score four goals in a remarkable 6–5 victory. Ernest Willimowski scored four goals for Poland and finished on the losing side.

• Dr Charles Dietz, Hungary's sole selector for the 1938 finals, said before the Hungarians played Switzerland in their quarter-finals match at Lille; 'If we don't beat the Swiss, I'll walk home to Hungary.' Dr Georges Sarosi, the Hungarian centre-forward, captain and a lawyer when he was not playing football, overheard and insisted on Dr Dietz putting his statement in writing. There were several frights for Dr Dietz before Hungary mastered the Swiss 2–0. But it was anything but a walkover!

• Italian skipper Peppino Meazza had that sinking feeling as he scored the semi-final penalty against Brazil that clinched a place in the 1938 Final. As he steered the spot-kick into the net his shorts, torn earlier in the game, slipped down to leave him exposed. His celebrating team-mates hid his blushes until a new pair were produced.

• Hungarian goalkeeper Antal Szabo startled visitors to the dressing-room after Hungary's defeat by Italy in the 1938 Final when he told them: 'I have never felt so proud in my life.' As his audience looked on dumbstruck, he explained: 'We may have lost the match but we have saved 11 lives. The Italian players received a telegram from Rome before the game which read, "Win or die!" Now they can go home as heroes.' As this was in the days of the Mussolini dictatorship, the story may not be so far-fetched as it sounds.

• With war clouds gathering over Europe, Jules Rimet – then President of FIFA and the man after whom the World Cup trophy was named – reclaimed the trophy from the Italian FA. He thought long and hard about where it would be safest, decided that the only place was the bedroom! For the duration of the Second World War the Jules Rimet Trophy nestled under his bed.!

• Italy were stunned to a 3–2 defeat by the amateurs of Sweden in their opening World Cup match in Sao Paulo in the 1950 finals. Italian clubs responded by signing up eight of the triumphant Swedish team. If you can't beat 'em, buy 'em . . . !

• The United States players believed like everybody else that they would be merely playing a walk-on part against the might of England in their 1950 group match at Belo Horizonte. Several of the American players stayed up until the early hours on the eve of the match and their Scots-born coach Bill Jeffrey told the Press: 'We're just hoping we can stop England mounting a cricket score.' One English football writer was asked by an American player: 'Have you brought a cribbage board to keep count of the English goals?' It is now history that the United States won 1–0. It was as if the Indians had upped and massacred John Wayne and his men!

• Yugoslav inside-left Rajko Mitic walked into an iron girder as he was leaving the dressing-room for the start of the 1950 match against Brazil at the Maracana Stadium. He gashed his forehead and knocked himself out. The 10 remaining players went out on to the pitch for the pre-match ceremony and then started to walk back to the dressing-room in a bid to delay the kick-off. Welsh referee Mervyn Griffiths insisted they start the game straightaway and so Brazil kicked off against 10 men. By the time the heavily-bandaged and still dazed Mitic joined the action Yugoslavia were a goal down and they were finally beaten 2–0. Later in his career, Mitic became manager of the Yugoslav national team.

• Austria beat Switzerland 7–5 in an astonishing quarter-finals match at Lausanne in the 1954 tournament. The Swiss came up with an unusual reason for some eccentric play by goalkeeper Eugene Parlier on a blistering-hot day. It was announced after the match that Parlier had been suffering from sunstroke.

• Juan Hohberg scored an eighty-seventh minute equaliser for Uruguay against Hungary in the 1954 semi-finals. His team-mates overdid the celebrating and goal hero Hohberg was knocked out under the weight of their congratulations. He recovered in time to join in the extra-time session during which he struck a shot against a post before Hungary forced a 4–2 victory.

• Scotland suddenly became the team without a manager when Andy Beattie announced his resignation after the Scots had gone down 1–0 to Austria in their opening match in the 1954 finals. Beattie felt that he was not being allowed to manage by the Scottish selectors.

• Northern Ireland, surprise qualifiers at the expense of Italy, brought humour as well as skill and endeavour to the 1958 finals. In trainer Gerry Morgan, a lovable little man with a Jimmy Durante profile and rakishly worn headgear, they had one of the great characters of the tournament. He regaled visitors from the world's Press corps to the Irish headquarters with a procession of blarney-based stories that sent them away happy if incredulous. One newspaperman wrote that the Irish players had trained on a diet of whisky and potato bread. Another reported that they were on a £1,000-a-man win bonus, when the actual figure was nearer £10. Another revealed to his readers that Danny Blanchflower and Jimmy McIlroy had been promised knighthoods if Northern Ireland won the World Cup. All the stories were planted by the straight-faced, mischievous Gerry Morgan. Skipper Danny Blanchflower told startled reporters that Northern Ireland's secret tactic was always 'to equalise before the opposition scores'. The Irish had a party after every match, win, lose or draw. An 'outsider' walked into a swinging party after Northern Ireland had been beaten 3–1 by Argentina. 'What are you celebrating?' he asked manager Peter Doherty. 'We're drowning our sorrows,' he said with a wide grin. The Irish laughed their way all the way into the quarter-finals.

• The 1958 semi-final between host country Sweden and West Germany was threatened with an abandonment before a ball had been kicked. West German officials arrived at the ground to find there were no seats for them in the main stand. Dr Pecos Bauwens, President of the German FA, issued an ultimatum that either the Swedes provide seats for his colleagues or he would withdraw the German team from the match. The game kicked off with everybody sitting comfortably!

• The biggest crowd the Argentinian players faced in 1958 was the one waiting for them at the airport in Buenos Aires on their arrival home. Thousands gathered at the airport to greet them with a shower of rotten tomatoes, stones and fruit in a show of disgust at their performances in the finals where they had been beaten 3–1 by West Germany and 6–1

DANNY BLANCHFLOWER . . . "We must equalise before the opposition score!"

• Swiss inside-forward Norbert Eschmann was brought down by a sliding tackle from West German half-back Horst Szymaniak early in their 1962 group match in Santiago. He was treated on the touchline for 17 minutes and then played through the rest of the game as a hobbling passenger. An X-ray after the match showed he had a fractured ankle.

• Pele was so pleased with the two-goal debut of his deputy Amarildo for Brazil against Spain in 1962 that he jumped fully clothed into the team bath after the match to congratulate him!

• Chilean midfield player Eladio Rojas was so excited when he scored what proved the winning goal against Russia in the 1962 quarter-finals that he first of all hugged Russian goalkeeper Lev Yashin and then the Dutch referee Leo Horn!

• In 1966 the World Cup had its first four-legged hero. The Jules Rimet Trophy was stolen while on exhibition at a stamp show in Central Hall, Westminster. There was a massive police and public hunt for the missing trophy and just when it looked as if football's Number One prize had disappeared into the smelter's pot it was unearthed by a dog

AMARILDO . . . Pele made a splash after his World Cup debut.

by Czechoslovakia. A mob also descended on the Argentinian FA headquarters and smashed windows and tore up fencing. In Argentina, they like to win!

• On the second day of the 1962 finals in Chile Yugoslav right-winger Muhamed Mujic had a running battle with Russian right-back Eduard Dubinsky that ended with Mujic kicking his opponent so hard that he broke his leg. The next day Mujic was sent home to Yugoslavia in disgrace and his home Association banned him from football for a year.

• The saddest moment in the 1962 finals came with Uruguay's defeat by Yugoslavia in a group match at Arica. Manuel Gonzales, a 17-year-old bellboy at the hotel where the Uruguayans were staying, was so upset over the defeat that he suffered a heart attack and died. Manuel had been so enthusiastic about the Uruguayan players that they had adopted him as their mascot. The entire Uruguayan squad attended Manuel's funeral and they insisted on paying all the expenses.

PICKLES . . . four-legged World Cup hero.

ANTONIO CARBAJAL . . . kissed the posts for luck.

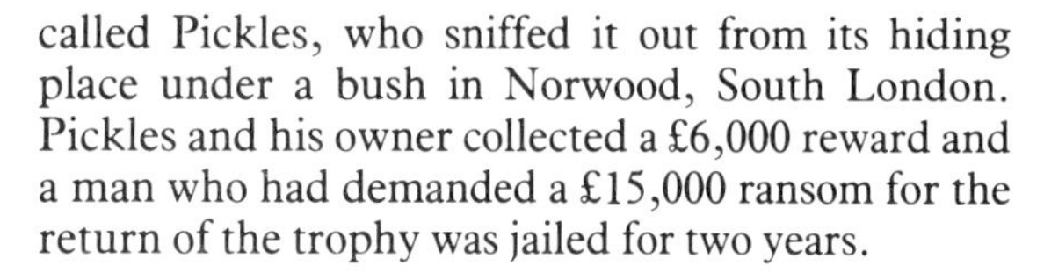

called Pickles, who sniffed it out from its hiding place under a bush in Norwood, South London. Pickles and his owner collected a £6,000 reward and a man who had demanded a £15,000 ransom for the return of the trophy was jailed for two years.

• The Mexican goalkeepers took the eye before the kick-off to their 1966 matches in the London group. Ignacio Calderon knelt in prayer beneath the crossbar just before the two matches in which he played and the veteran Antonio Carbajal kissed both his goalposts for luck. He was rewarded with a goalless draw against Uruguay.

• West German star Helmut Haller had a reputation for being theatrical because of the way he writhed on the floor after every tackle. But against Uruguay he had the sympathy of even the boldest men when he collapsed to the ground in obvious agony. A Uruguayan, on the blind side of English referee Jim Finney, had seized and squeezed his testicles!

• Mexican fans went wild with delight when their team won their second match of the 1970 tournament against El Salvador at the Aztec Stadium in Mexico City. Within minutes of the final whistle the entire city had been brought to a standstill as thousands of people took to the streets to start an impromptu carnival. A giant 12-foot fibreglass football that had been decorating the FIFA headquarters in the city centre was wrenched from the roof of the hotel and dribbled away into the night, never to be seen again. It was carnival time again after Mexico had beaten Belgium in their third match and this time the city was brought to an almost complete, chaotic halt until late into the night. Press buses carrying reporters anxious to cable their stories back home should have taken 40 minutes from the Aztec Stadium to the Press headquarters. The journey finally took four hours!

• There were unproven stories that Brazilian referee Airton Viera de Moraes had made approaches to officials of Uruguay and Sweden offering to favour them in their 1970 group match in return for money. After being interviewed by Sir Stanley Rous, President of FIFA, Moraes denied the accusation but was switched from the match at the last minute. Uruguay reacted by saying they would play the match only under protest and claimed that Moraes being taken off the match was an implication against them. Rous later announced that he was satisfied that de Moraes had been the victim of a plot.

• To relax before one of their 1970 group matches the England players went to a rodeo in Mexico City and watched bulls being ridden. Somebody asked West Brom striker Jeff Astle if he would ride one of the bulls for £1,000. 'For £1,000, I'd milk the bloody thing,' said Jeff, famous for his one-line jokes.

• The West German players celebrated their progress through to the quarter-finals of the 1970 tournament by throwing team manager Helmut Schoen, fully clothed, into the swimming pool at their hotel headquarters. 'It is not so good for me but very good for the team spirit,' said a dripping-wet Herr Schoen.

• Alan Ball was so bitterly disappointed by England's 3–2 defeat by West Germany in the 1970 quarter-finals that he threw his tournament medal out of his hotel bedroom window.

• Brazilian fans, many of them Press photographers and radio interviewers, excitedly mobbed the Brazil players after they had beaten Italy in the 1970 Final to win the Jules Rimet Trophy outright. Rivelino, one of Brazil's heroes, collapsed under the weight of their felicitations and had to be carried to the dressing-room on a stretcher.

HELMUT SCHOEN . . . dripping with delight.

• Brazil skipper Carlos Alberto was so hemmed in by celebrating team-mates and fans as he paraded the Jules Rimet Trophy after the 1970 Final that he failed to notice that the gold top of the trophy had fallen to the ground. Brazilian reserve Dario retrieved it just as a young spectator was making for the exit with his unexpected souvenir!

• Tostao gave his Brazilian shirt and his World Cup winners' medal to the surgeon in Houston, Texas, who had performed two operations on a detached retina in his eye during the year immediately before the 1970 finals.

• The West Germans staged a spectacular opening ceremony to the 1974 finals that involved meticulous organisation. But they had overlooked one minor detail. As Brazil and Yugoslavia lined up for the kick-off to the opening match in the stadium at Frankfurt, the referee delayed the start while embarrassed officials hustled around the pitch putting in the corner and centre-line flags

• Haiti were involved in a controversial qualifying match on their way into the 1974 finals. They staged all the matches in their qualifying group in their own country and one of them, against Trinidad, was curious to say the least. Trinidad had the ball in the Haitian net four times and every 'goal' was disallowed by Enriquez, a referee from El Salvador. Haiti won 2–1 and went to Munich. Enriquez was subsequently suspended.

• Holland threatened a walk-off protest before a ball had been kicked in the 1978 World Cup Final against Argentina. Daniel Passarella objected to the Italian referee Sergio Gonella about a small plaster on Rene Van de Kerkhof's hand. It was protecting bones that he had damaged in an early match against Iran. Passarella suggested it was dangerous. Dutch midfield player Johan Neeskens, who speaks Spanish, told the Argentinian captain: 'If Rene goes, we all go.' Gonella finally persuaded Van der Kerkhof to return to the dressing-room to have a soft cover placed over the plaster and delayed the kick-off until he came back on to the pitch. It was an unnecessary piece of Argentinian gamesmanship and may have accounted for the match often boiling over with fierce tackles and vicious fouls.

OFF! OFF! OFF!

Mario De las Casas, Peru captain and right-back, reluctantly took a place in the World Cup record book in one of the opening matches of the 1930 finals. He was ordered off for consistent violent play against Romania, the first player to get marching orders in the World Cup. It took five minutes of protest and pleading before he was forced to accept the decision by the Chilean referee who had given him several warnings for violent play. Romanian right-back Adalbert Steiner had his leg broken during a brawling match but De las Casas was not involved. He was the first in a long line of World Cup players sent for an early bath . . .

1934 Markos (Hungary) v Austria.

1938 Zeze and Machados (Brazil) and Riha (Czechoslovakia), all in the same match. *(See Battle of Bordeaux.)*

1950 No players were ordered off.

1954 Bozsik (Hungary) and Nilton Santos and Tozzi (Brazil), all in the same match. *(See Battle of Berne.)*

1958 Bubernik (Czechoslovakia) v Northern Ireland; Sipos (Hungary) v Wales; Juskowiak (West Germany) v Sweden.

1962 This was the blackest year for sendings off, with six players ordered to the dressing-rooms: Ferrini and David (Italy) v Chile *(see Battle of Santiago);* Popovic (Yugoslavia) and Cabrera (Uruguay), for fighting each other; Landa (Chile) and Garrincha (Brazil), following separate incidents in their semi-final. All the players with the exception of Garrincha were punished with a one-match suspension but the Brazilian star was let off with a warning after the Brazilian Prime Minister had sent a dramatic telegram to Sir Stanley Rous that read: 'Brazilian government expects FIFA authorities to overlook any misunderstandings and allow the full team to play Final specially that extraordinary athlete Garrincha whose discipline is renowned throughout the world.' FIFA's disciplinary committee got round their problem by deciding the referee had not clearly seen the incident and had sent Garrincha off after consulting a linesman. Most people in the stadium saw Garrincha clearly kick Chilean defender Rojas but the referee's report said he had 'elbowed' him. So tournament star Garrincha was cleared to play a prominent part in Brazil's World Cup victory over Czechoslovakia in the Final.

1966 Five players were sent off during the finals in England, four of them during matches against West Germany – Albrecht (Argentina), Silva and Troche (Uruguay) and Chislenko (Russia). The exception was Argentinian captain Antonio Rattin who was ordered off in a sensational quarter-finals match against England at Wembley. He appeared to be almost trying to referee the game as he argued and protested at every decision against Argentina.

RUDOLF KREITLIN . . . sent Rattin off at Wembley in 1966.

Finally the real referee, Herr Rudolf Kreitlin of West Germany, ran out of patience with Rattin's arrogant and insulting behaviour and ordered him to leave the pitch in the thirty-sixth minute. The tall Rattin, a towering inferno, flatly refused to go and the game was held up for 10 minutes while FIFA officials led by referees' chief Ken Aston tried to restore law and order. Just as it looked as if Rattin's team-mates were going to walk off in protest Rattin at last agreed to make a slow, lonely walk to the dressing-room. Herr Kreitlin later revealed that though he could not speak Spanish he could understand the look on Rattin's face and it convinced him that the Argentinian captain had to go.

1970 Despite all the fears of this developing into a violent tournament, there was not a single player ordered off.

1974 Caszely (Chile) v West Germany; Castillo (Uruguay) v Holland; Pereira (Brazil) v Holland.

1978 Toroscik and Nyilasi (Hungary) v Argentina.

COMMENTS

'I was sitting on the touchline that day and had no doubt that the referee was right to send Rattin off. He was trying to run the game and to dictate to the referee what decisions to make. I just couldn't understand the Argentinian tactics. They seemed to want to turn the match into a rough-house instead of concentrating on their football. Argentina were the most talented team in the tournament but they had no control over their temperament. There was a nasty sequel when a mob of their players tried to fight their way into the England dressing-room after the match. I remember taking refuge behind Jack Charlton, he being the biggest player in our team!'

OLYMPIC HEROES

Seven of the Uruguayan team that won the first World Cup Final in 1930 were also members of the gold-medal-winning team at the 1928 Olympics: skipper Jose Nasazzi, Jose Andrade, Alvaro Gestido, Hector Scarone, Pedro Cea, Lorenzo Fernandez and Hector Castro. For Nasazzi, Andrade, Scarone and Cea it was a unique hat-trick because they also won Olympic gold medals with Uruguay in 1924.

In 1938, Italian full-back partners Alfredo Foni and Pietro Rava and half-back Locatelli added World Cup winners' medals to the Olympic gold medals they had won in the 1936 Berlin Olympics.

Swedes Sune Andersson, Knut Nordahl, Stellan Nillson and Erik Nillson won Bronze medals in the 1950 World Cup finals to go with the Olympic golds they won with Sweden in the 1948 Olympics in London.

In 1954, nine Hungarians added World Cup silver medals to the Olympic golds they had won at Helsinki in 1952: Gyula Grocis, Jena Buzansky, Gyula Lorant, Mihaly Lantos, Josef Bozsik, Nandor Hidegkuti, Sandor Kocsis, Ferenc Puskas and Zoltan Czibor.

ORSI, Raimondo (Argentina and Italy)

Born in Argentina in 1901 of Italian parents Orsi starred on the left wing for the Argentinian team that won the 1924 and 1928 Olympic titles. He was persuaded to join Juventus and flourished in the Italian League. His dual nationality meant that Italy were able to play him in the 1934 World Cup and he scored a crucial goal that helped them beat Czechoslovakia in the Final. He scored 13 goals in 35 appearances for Italy.

OVERATH, Wolfgang (West Germany)

A schoolboy, youth, under-23 and full international (playing against Martin Peters at all levels), Wolfgang Overath was a skilful midfield schemer for West Germany in three World Cup tournaments. He was a runner-up in the 1966 Final against England, was outstanding for the West German team that finished third in 1970 and had the most memorable moments of his career when he collected a winners' medal in 1974. Born on 29 September 1943, he started his career with local club Siegburg before joining Cologne. He made his international debut against Sweden in 1963 and retired from international football after his eightieth appearance for West Germany in the 1974 World Cup Final.

COMMENTS

'Overath was a smooth, unspectacular player who knitted the West German team together with his neat, precise passes. He had a beautifully educated right foot and gave a superb service to the strikers. I rated his great rival Gunther Netzer the more gifted player but Overath was time and again preferred to him in midfield because he was more consistent and reliable.'

OWN GOALS

Swiss defender Ernst Loertscher was the first player to score an 'own' goal in the World Cup finals. He turned the ball past his own goalkeeper in a first round replay against West Germany in Paris in 1938 but the Swiss had the last laugh by winning 4–2.

There was a record haul of 'own' goals in the 1954 finals. Five players experienced the nightmare moment of putting the ball into their own net: Cardenas (Mexico) v France; Jimmy Dickinson (England) v Belgium; Horvat (Yugoslavia) v West Germany; Hanappi (Austria) v Switzerland; Cruz (Uruguay) v Austria.

Bulgarian defender Ivan Vutzov created a record in the 1966 finals in England that will always haunt him. He put the ball past his own goalkeeper in successive matches. His first was a spectacular

header that gave Portugal a gift goal at Old Trafford. Four days later on the same ground he again turned the ball into his own net to put Hungary on the way to a victory that eliminated Bulgaria from the tournament.

PARAGUAY

Their World Cup finals record:

1930 USA (0–3), Belgium (1–0).

1950 Sweden (2–2), Italy (0–2).

1958 France (3–7), Scotland (3–2), Yugoslavia (3–3).

Summary: P7 W2 D2 L3 F12 A19

PASSARELLA, Daniel (Argentina)

Typifying the modern, athletic defender, Passarella has the speed, stamina and skill to switch to an

DANIEL PASSARELLA . . . after collecting the World Cup in 1978.

attacking, adventurous role. Captain of the triumphant 1978 Argentinian team, he was a steadying influence at the heart of the defence and used his left foot to trigger attacks with intelligently placed passes. Born in 1953, Passarella is an aggressive competitor who gives strength and steel to the River Plate defence. He has played more than 50 matches for Argentina and his performances in the 1978 World Cup established him as one of the world's outstanding attacking defenders.

PELE, Edson Arantes do Nascimento (Brazil)

PELE . . . rather pleased with his goal against Italy in the 1970 World Cup Final. ▶

The one and only Pele collected 12 goals in four World Cup final tournaments. He is the only player to have been a member of three World Cup winning teams (1958/62/70), although he missed the final stages of the 1962 tournament because of a pulled muscle. His total appearances including his two matches in 1966 were 14 and he scored in the 1958 and the 1970 Finals.

Born in near poverty in Tres Coracoes, Bauru, on 23 October 1940, Pele came under the influence of former Brazilian World Cup player Waldemar de Brito while playing for his local team of Noroeste. De Brito recommended him to Santos where he quickly emerged as an international star, making his debut for Brazil at the age of 16 and getting world-wide acclaim at the age of 17 for his magnificent performances in the 1958 World Cup finals

He scored 1,216 goals in 1,254 matches from 7 September 1956 until his retirement on 2 October 1974. His peak year for goals was 1958 when he scored 139 times. In 1975 he made a comeback with New York Cosmos, giving soccer in the States the kick of life. He made a farewell appearance against Santos in New Jersey before a sell-out crowd on 1 October 1977. It was Pele's one thousand, three hundred and sixty-third match and he naturally marked it with a goal to bring his career total to 1,281.

COMMENTS

'In a word, Pele was a genius. I'm sure he could have been a world-class gymnast had he not chosen football as his sport. He had wonderful spring, perfect balance, could shoot with either foot, was as brave as a lion and had tremendous vision. The man had *everything*. If Maradona is valued at £5 million, Pele at his peak would be worth £10 million.'

PENALTIES

There will never be a more dramatic penalty award than the one given by English referee Jack Taylor in the very first minute of the 1974 Final. Not a single German player had touched the ball when Johan Cruyff was brought down by Uli Hoeness as he raced into the penalty area following a lightning-fast, 15-pass move by the Dutch masters. Johan Neeskens scored from the spot. West Germany's equaliser on the way to a 2–1 victory came from a penalty by Paul Breitner. They were the first penalties awarded in a World Cup Final.

JACK TAYLOR... awarded a first-minute penalty in the 1974 World Cup final.

The first penalties awarded in a World Cup match came in the opening tournament in Uruguay in 1930 and they came in an astonishing burst. Bolivian referee Ulysses Saucedo gave no fewer than five penalties as Argentina spot-kicked their way to a 6–3 victory over Mexico.

There have been four penalty goals in semi-final matches. Italian skipper Peppino Meazza scored from the spot just a split second before his torn shorts fell down. Literally a split second! Fritz Walter scored two goals from the penalty spot for West Germany against Austria in the 1954 semi-final. His brother Otmar headed two more goals in Germany's 6–1 victory.

Eusebio scored four times from the penalty spot for Portugal during the 1966 finals, twice against North Korea, and against England in the semi-final and against Russia in the play-off for third place.

Robbie Rensenbrink also scored four goals from penalty kicks for Holland during the 1978 tournament, two against Iran and one each against Scotland and Austria.

Johan Neeskens converted two spot-kicks for

Holland against Bulgaria in the 1978 finals as well as his history-making penalty against West Germany in the first minute of the Final.

Ron Flowers was England's top scorer in the 1962 finals with two goals, both from the penalty spot – the first against Hungary and the second against Argentina.

England's Tom Finney scored one of the World Cup's coolest penalties against Russia in 1958. Faced by great Russian goalkeeper Lev Yashin and nursing a leg injury, Finney expertly steered the ball into the back of the net for a late equaliser that rescued England from what had seemed certain defeat.

There have been a spate of missed penalties in World Cup matches, including:

1934 De Brito, the Brazilian who later discovered Pele, against Spain.

1954 Robert Koerner (Austria) against Switzerland in a match won 7–5 by the Austrians.

TOM FINNEY . . . cool on the spot for England.

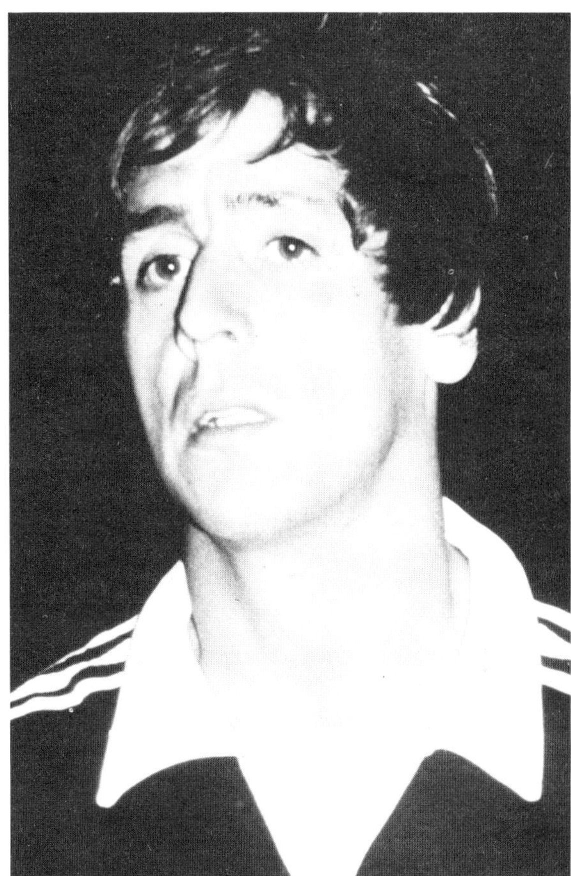

DON MASSON . . . missed a penalty against Peru.

1958 John Hewie (Scotland) who shot his spot-kick against a post in a match won 2–1 by France.

1978 Don Masson (Scotland) had his penalty saved by Peruvian goalkeeper Quiroga; the score was then 1–1 and Peru went on to win 3–1. Kazimierz Deyna (Poland), playing in his one-hundredth international match, had his spot-kick saved by Argentine goalkeeper Ubaldo Fillol.

In the 1974 tournament, Poland's unconventional Jan Tomaszewski became the first goalkeeper to make two penalty saves, the first against Tapper (Switzerland) and the second against Hoeness (West Germany).

The most hotly disputed penalty in World Cup history came during Mexico's match against France in Geneva in 1954. Spanish referee Manuel Ansensi was protected by French players and police as a posse of incensed Mexican players chased him round the pitch after he had awarded France a late penalty. Raymond Kopa scored to give the French a 3–2 victory. The referee was escorted off by police at the end as Mexican players renewed their attempts to assault him.

Allan Clarke, the Leeds striker who became manager of the club, is the only player to have scored a World Cup goal from the penalty spot in his first international match. Manager Sir Alf Ramsey asked for a volunteer to take any necessary penalties before the 1970 match against Czechoslovakia. Allan boldly elected himself despite it being his debut and coolly netted the only goal of the game early in the second half.

PERU

Their record in World Cup finals:

1930 Romania (1–3), Uruguay (0–1).

1970 Bulgaria (3–2), Morocco (3–0), West Germany (1–3), Brazil (2–4, quarter-finals).

1978 Scotland (3–1), Holland (0–0), Iran (4–1), Brazil (0–3), Poland (0–1), Argentina (0–6).

Summary: P12 W4 D1 L7 A25

Peru were involved in a controversial match with eventual champions Argentina in their last appearance in the 1978 finals. Argentina kicked off knowing they needed four goals to reach the Final and against a team that had previously looked one of the most skilful and enterprising in the tournament. Peru simply surrendered against the aggressive Argentinians and were hammered 6–0. Brazil, pipped for a place in the Final were bitterly disappointed and there were all sorts of allegations flying against the Peruvians, particularly as their goalkeeper, Quiroga, was born in Argentina. Quiroga was forced to go to the length of having an open letter published in which he refuted allegations that the result had been in any way fixed. Claudio Coutinho, Brazil's manager, was outspoken against Peru and said that none of their players could ever have pride again when standing on the pitch listening to their national anthem. The game and Peru's performance left a scar on the tournament.

PETERS, Martin (England)

A high-quality player whose subtle skills were always more appreciated by his fellow professionals than the public, Peters had the greatest moment of his distinguished career in the 1966 World Cup Final when he shot England into a 2–1 lead. He played with precision and imagination for West Ham, Tottenham, Norwich City and Sheffield

MARTIN PETERS . . . the 'Gentle Executioner.'

United, with whom he was briefly manager. Born in Plaistow, West Ham, on 8 November 1943, Peters made 67 appearances including nine matches in the World Cup final tournaments of 1966 and 1970. This 'Gentle Executioner' stole 20 goals for England.

COMMENTS

'Like me, Martin learnt the game on the playing fields of Dagenham. He was a thoroughbred from the top of his head to the tip of his toes and was an absolute master at making blind-side runs that time and again caught defences napping. His imaginative runs from midfield played an important part in making England a power in the mid-1960s. Alf Ramsey, another Dagenhamite, described him as being 10 years ahead of his time. He was a great player of the modern game.'

PIOLA, Silvio (Italy)

The most prolific goal-scorer in Italian football history, Piola was the outstanding centre-forward in the 1938 finals in France. His two goals helped lift Italy to their 4–2 victory over Hungary in the Final in Paris. Born at Robbio Lomellina on 29 September 1913, he had a long and eventful career that included 32 international appearances and skilled service with Pro Vercelli, Lazio, Torino, Juventus and Novara. He scored twice in his debut for Italy against Austria in 1937 and made his final international appearance against England in Florence in 1952 at the age of 38. At the close of his career he became manager of the Italian under-23 team. In February 1951, he notched the goal that finally beat Peppino Meazza's record aggregate Italian League haul of 355 goals.

POLAND

Their World Cup finals record:

1938 Brazil (5–6). This was the match in which Leonidas da Silva (Brazil) and Ernest Willimowski (Poland) each scored four goals, with the Poles being eliminated after a nail-biting period of extra-time.

1974 Argentina (3–2), Haiti (7–0), Italy (2–1), Sweden (1–0), Yugoslavia (2–1), West Germany (0–1), Brazil (1–0). Finished third.

1978 West Germany (0–0), Tunisia (1–0), Mexico (3–0), Argentina (0–2), Peru (1–0), Brazil (1–3).

Summary: P14 W9 D1 L4 F27 A17

PLANICKA, Frantisek (Czechoslovakia)

One of Europe's most accomplished goalkeepers between the wars, Planicka kept Czechoslovakia in the 1934 World Cup finals with a procession of magnificent saves. Yet in the Final it was his failure to 'read' a curling shot from Raimondo Orsi that cost the Czechs any chance of holding Italy.

Born in 1904, Planicka played in 74 internationals for Czechoslovakia and captained both his country and his club side Slavia Prague, with whom he won eight League championship medals between 1924 and 1937. He was again Czechoslovakia's last line of defence in the 1938 World Cup, breaking an arm in the brawling quarter-finals match with Brazil. Planicka continued to play at local League level until his mid-fifties.

PLUSKAL, Svatopluk (Czechoslovakia)

This strong, reliable defender played for Czechoslovakia in three World Cup final tournaments, first at centre-half in 1958 and then as an anchorman half-back in 1958 and 1962.He was rewarded for his consistency in 1962 when he collected a runners-up medal with the Czechs after their defeat in the Final by Brazil. Born in Zlin in 1931, Pluskal played 58 times for Czechoslovakia and won seven League Championship medals with Dukla Prague.

POPLUHAR, Jan (Czechoslovakia)

This big, bald centre-half stood at the heart of the Czechoslovakian defence like a man mountain defying anybody to come past him. His immense strength mixed with solid technique made him one of Europe's most formidable defenders of his era. He played in the 1958 World Cup finals and was a key man in defence when Czechoslovakia reached the 1962 Final. Born in 1935, Popluhar gave magnificent service to Slovan Bratislava before winding down his career with Lyons in the French League.

COMMENTS

'Pluskal, Popluhar and Masopust were the three men mainly responsible for Czechoslovakia's success in the 1962 World Cup. They balanced each other perfectly and were extremely competitive as well as technically sound. I can't say it was ever a pleasure playing against them for England and Tottenham but they certainly earned my respect. Each of them autographed my shins at one time or another!'

PORTUGAL

Portugal created an excellent impression in their only World Cup finals appearance in 1966 when they finished third. In their group matches they beat Hungary (3–1), Bulgaria (3–0) and Brazil (3–1) to qualify for their memorable quarter-final against the North Koreans. Portugal were 3–0 down against the Koreans when Eusebio took over to score four goals and create a fifth. They were beaten 2–1 by England in a classic semi-final at Wembley and then conquered Russia 2–1 in a play-off for third place. Their team in the semi-final was: Pereira, Festa, Baptista, Carlos, Hilario, Graca, Coluna, Augusto, Eusebio, Torres, Simoes.

POZZO, Vittorio (Italy)

In a 20-year span as manager of the Italian team, Pozzo twice lifted football's supreme prize, the World Cup. After helping form the famous Torino football club, Pozzo came to England to study. He became deeply impressed by the Manchester United team and in particular the attacking centre-half play of Charlie Roberts. When he returned to Italy he managed the national team that competed in the 1912 Olympics and after the war evolved tactics based on ideas nurtured while watching Manchester United. He built the Italian team around an attacking centre-half and was rewarded for his vision and imagination with World Cup victories in 1934 and 1938. Following his retirement in 1948, this highly intelligent, self-confident man became a respected football journalist and his articles revealed the authority and powers of reasoning that made him a legend in the game between the wars.

PUSKAS, Ferenc (Hungary)

With his stunningly powerful left-foot shot and his ability to be a thought and a deed ahead of most defenders, Ferenc Puskas was probably *the* most influential player in the magnificent Hungarian team of the 1950s that went four years and 29 games without a single defeat. The unbeaten run sadly ended in the 1954 World Cup Final when Puskas insisted on playing despite an ankle injury that robbed him of much of his fire and flair. After the 1956 Hungarian Uprising, Puskas added to his reputation as one of the greatest players of all time by becoming a front-line master with Real Madrid for whom he scored four goals in the 1960 European Cup Final and three in the 1962 Final.

Born in Budapest in 1926, Puskas was often Hungarian captain, winning 84 international caps before his defection in 1956. He was top Hungarian League marksman in 1947, 1950 and 1953, and became known as 'The Galloping Major' in the Honved team that consisted of players who had been commissioned in the Hungarian army. Puskas led the 'Magical Magyars' to their historic 6–3 and 7–1 victories over England in 1953–54, collected a gold medal in the 1952 Olympics and then had the biggest disappointment of his career in the 1954 World Cup Final. He scored Hungary's first goal but had another ruled off-side just as he began to celebrate what he thought was a late equaliser against West Germany.

FERENC PUSKAS . . . 'could unlock a safe door with his left foot.'

With Real Madrid, he struck up a devastating partnership with Alfredo di Stefano and was top Spanish League scorer in 1960, 1961, 1963 and 1964. He played for Spain in three World Cup final matches in 1962 but was then 36 and slowed to a stroll by a spreading waistline. At the end of his brilliant and eventful playing career he switched to management and led Panathanaikos of Athens to the 1971 European Cup Final.

COMMENTS

'I grew up idolising Puskas and had the honour and privilege of playing against him for England against the Rest of the World at Wembley in 1963. I have never seen a better left foot than his. He could unlock a safe door with it and also had the power to dynamite it open. "The Galloping Major" would have to be high in anybody's top 10 list of all-time great players. He was a complete master of the game. His 85 goals in 84 international matches for Hungary is surely proof of his genius.'

QUIROGA, Ramon (Peru)

Though his goalkeeping was not quite out of the coaching manual, Ramon Quiroga emerged as one of the most popular of all performers in the 1978 finals in Argentina. He was to say the least unconventional in his play, often coming well outside his penalty area to encourage his team-mates and play the ball with his feet. Nicknamed *'El Loco'*, he saved a penalty against Scotland, shut out Holland, made three saves against Poland that were out of this world and was booked by English referee Pat Partridge for a rugby tackle on Poland's Grzegorz Lato inside *Poland*'s half of the field.

He became even more popular with the Argentinian fans when he let in six goals in Peru's crucial final match that Argentina used as a stepping stone to the Final. There were widespread stories that the match had been fixed as Quiroga was Argentinian by birth. He pleaded his innocence and had a full letter of explanation for Peru's collapse against Argentina published in South American newspapers. The last line of defence for Cristal in Peru, Quiroga was one of the most talked-about players of the tournament both for his eccentric behaviour and a series of incredible reflex saves. But those reflexes were not working against Argentina in the match that really mattered.

RAHN, Helmut (West Germany)

A last-minute choice for West Germany's 1954 squad, this power-propelled right-winger responded with the two goals that turned likely defeat into glorious victory against Hungary in the dramatic Final. He was on tour in Uruguay with his club side Rot-Weiss Essen and considering an offer to join Uruguayan champions Penarol when German team manager Sepp Herberger summoned him to join the World Cup action.

Born in 1929, Rahn was slowed by weight problems after his triumph in 1954 but he went on a crash diet to get himself fit for the 1958 finals and emerged as West Germany's top scorer in the tournament with six goals in six matches. He won 40 international caps between 1951 and 1960, and collected a German cup-winners' medal and a League championship medal with Rot-Weiss Essen before transferring to Cologne in 1959.

RAMSEY, Sir Alf (England)

This former international full-back was knighted for masterminding England's 1966 World Cup triumph. He was such a calculating, tactically minded right-back that his team-mates in the famous push-and-run Tottenham team of the 1950s nicknamed him 'The General'. After playing 32 times for England, Ramsey retired in 1955 and switched with tremendous success to management with Ipswich Town. He led them from the Third Division (South) to the Second and First Division championships in successive seasons, a title double that he also achieved as a player with Spurs. Appointed successor to Walter Winterbottom as England team manager in October 1962, he brought a new era of professionalism to the international set-up.

Born in Dagenham on 22 January 1920, Ramsey burdened himself with the prophecy that England would win the World Cup in 1966, and then came up with the tactics and the team to make it come true. His full record as England manager was: P105, W67, D24, L14, F213, A90. He was sacked after England's failure to qualify for the 1974 World Cup finals. Sir Alf, who started his playing career with Southampton, has since had a short, unsuccessful spell as manager of Birmingham City.

COMMENTS

'There have been few people able to match Alf as a strategist. The secret of his success as England manager was evolving the right tactics to suit the strength of his players and also to camouflage the weaknesses. He had total recall of every match and every player he ever watched and always had the courage of his convictions. Despite what some people think, I always had a great respect for Alf and, had his public relations been better, I feel he would still be England's manager, a job he did better than anybody.'

SIR ALF RAMSEY . . . enjoying the sunshine of Mexico before the shadow of defeat by West Germany in the 1970 World Cup.

RATTIN, Antonio (Argentina)

A giant in size and talent, Rattin will always be best (or worst) remembered for his arrogant behaviour when ordered off during Argentina's 1966 World Cup quarter-final against England at Wembley. It is a pity that this incident clouded a career in which he revealed he had the ability and artistry to be compared with the finest players in the world.

Born in 1937, Rattin proved himself a natural leader on the football field and became captain of Boca Juniors and Argentina. He played one game against England in the 1962 World Cup finals and many people considered him the man most likely to collect the World Cup in 1966 until his loss of self-control in the quarter-finals. Rattin was at his most devastating when playing an attacking role from a midfield base but could also be effective in defence where a ruthless nature often boiled to the surface. He played a record 352 League games for Boca Juniors where he was idolised.

◀ RAMON QUIROGA . . . chaired off after his penalty save helped Peru beat Scotland in the 1978 World Cup finals.

COMMENTS

'I played against Tony Rattin when we beat Argentina 3–1 in the 1962 World Cup and again two years later in Rio when Argentina were 1–0 winners. I have rarely seen a more impressive character on a football pitch. He had tremendous presence, not only because of his giant frame but also because he was a beautifully balanced and inventive player. Yet he somehow epitomised Argentian football. He had all the talent in the world but a temperament that was volcanic. He was likely to erupt at any moment and, sadly for him and Argentina, the big boil-up came in the most important match of his career.'

RAYNOR, George (England and Sweden)

A little-known player in England with Rotherham and Aldershot, this slight, bubbling Yorkshireman became one of the world's most respected coaches who shaped and steered the Swedish team that finished runners-up to Brazil in the 1958 World Cup Final. He had given notice of his organisational ability when he plotted Sweden's path to third place in the 1950 finals. After an unhappy spell managing Italy, he returned to Sweden and by recruiting all the top Swedish exiles managed to piece together a team that could challenge the very best in the world. His triumph in 1958 brought pleasure and pride to the Football Association who had recommended him to the Swedish FA back in 1946 after he had impressed with his coaching methods in far-off Baghdad. Incredibly, his talent was ignored in England and when he returned home looking for a job the best he could get was manager of Skegness. His achievements with Sweden were surely worthy of recognition by a major League Club.

REFEREES

The referee for each of the World Cup finals:

1930 John Langenus (Belgium).
1934 Ingemar Eklind (Sweden).
1938 Georges Capdeville (France).
1950 (deciding match): George Reader (England).
1954 Bill Ling (England).
1958 Maurice Guige (France).
1962 Nikolai Latychev (Russia).
1966 Georg Dienst (Switzerland).
1970 Rudi Glockner (East Germany).
1974 Jack Taylor (England).
1978 Sergio Gonella (Italy).

There has yet to be a World Cup without at least one rumpus involving a referee. Here is a collection of some of the most controversial incidents:

Brazilian referee Almeida Rego caused a near-riot in one of the very first World Cup final matches in Uruguay in 1930. France were pressing for an equaliser as Argentina clung to their 1–0 lead when Senhor Rego blew the final whistle just as French left-winger Marcel Langiller was shaping to shoot at the end of a 50-yard run. Hundreds of Argentinian fans came dashing on to the pitch to celebrate their team's victory. While all this was going on referee Rego was being surrounded by protesting French officials arguing that he had blown the whistle six minutes too early. Rego's linesmen confirmed it and so he had to order mounted police to clear the pitch and instruct the players to come back from the dressing-room to complete the match. Argentinian inside-left Roberto Ciero fainted when he was told he had to return to the pitch. It took police and armed guards nearly half an hour to clear the playing area and then the two teams played out the last six minutes without futher score.

Hungarian referee Paul Hertzka lost control of the 1938 quarter-finals match between Brazil and Czechoslovakia. He sent off three players and another three had to go to hospital for treatment for serious injuries. The teams finished level at 1–1 after extra-time and, not surprisingly, there was a change of referee for the replay. *(See Battle of Bordeaux.)*

A posse of protesting Italian players chased Brazilian referee Mario Viana round and round the pitch after he had refused to disallow a disputed goal by Switzerland in their 1954 match. Senhor Viana finally ran right off the pitch and refused to resume the match until the fuming Italian players had calmed down.

England's Arthur Ellis was given a police escort at the end of the brutal brawl between Brazil and Hungary in the 1954 quarter-finals. He sent off three players in a match that was always vicious and

ARTHUR ELLIS . . . the man in the middle of the 'Battle of Berne.'

often violent. Despite protests about his refereeing from the Brazilians, most neutral observers considered that Ellis had handled an 'impossible' match with commendable dignity. 'But for the firm refereeing of Mr Ellis,' one Swiss journalist recorded, 'this disgraceful match would never have run its course.' *(See Battle of Berne.)*

Russian referee Nikolai Latychev would not win any popularity polls in Hungary. In 1958 he sent off Hungarian centre-half Ferenc Sipos after a succession of fouls on Welsh hero John Charles. Four years later in the 1962 quarter-finals, the same Nikolai Latychev turned down what Hungary claimed was a perfectly legitimate equaliser by Lajos Tichy against Czechoslovakia. The Czechs won the match 1–0.

Ken Aston, a primary school headmaster from Ilford in Essex, was the man in the middle of what he described as an 'uncontrollable' match when Chile played Italy in 1962. The Italians had two players sent off and later accused Mr Aston of being 'hostile and provocative'. To make the match even more memorable for the referee, he injured an Achilles tendon and limped painfully through the remainder of his World Cup matches. *(See Battle of Santiago.)*

Argentina's players threatened to walk off in protest when West German referee Rudolf Kreitlin sent off their captain Antonio Rattin in the 1966 quarter-finals against England at Wembley. It was Ken Aston, then chief of the referees' delegation, who came on to the pitch to act as peacemaker. *(See Off! Off! Off!)*

KEN ASTON . . . the man in the middle of the 'Battle of Santiago.'

Egyptian referee Hussain Kandil reduced the El Salvador players to tears with an extraordinary decision that led to Mexico taking a 1–0 lead a minute before half-time in their 1970 match. The referee clearly awarded El Salvador a free-kick but it was a Mexican player who took it. While the El Salvador players stood protesting, Kandil waved 'play on' and the Mexicans scored. There were extraordinary scenes as some El Salvador players chased the referee while others fell to the pitch openly weeping. One of them kicked the ball into the crowd and the referee blew for half-time with El Salvador refusing to take any further part in the match. They were persuaded to come out for the second half but lacked their earlier fight, and they slumped to a 4–0 defeat.

Argentinian referee Angel Coerezza was more of a devil as far as Belgium were concerned when they faced Mexico in 1970. The only goal of the game came from a penalty that few neutral observers felt should have been awarded. Mexican striker Javier Valdivia appeared to fall over as he reached the Belgian penalty area and to everybody's astonishment Senor Coerezza pointed to the penalty spot. Play was held up for two minutes while the referee was besieged by protesting Belgian players. When all the arguing was over, Mexican skipper Gustavo Pena steered the spot-kick into the net to put Mexico through to the quarter-finals.

Welshman Clive Thomas, a referee who appears to have been a constant companion of controversy, caused fierce argument when he blew the final whistle just as what would have been Brazil's winning goal was on its way into the Swedish net in an eventful 1978 match. A corner-kick from Nelhino was in the air as Thomas signalled the end of the match. His whistle was still to his lips as Zico headed the ball past the Swedish goalkeeper who claimed he relaxed as he heard the whistle. Despite strong Brazilian protests the final score remained at 1–1.

RENSENBRINK, Robbie (Holland)

This flying Dutchman established himself as one of Europe's outstanding wingers while with Anderlecht in Belgium. It was his speed and skill on the right flank for Anderlecht that destroyed the West Ham defence in the 1976 European Cup Winners' Cup. Born in 1948, Rensenbrink first

ROBBIE RENSENBRINK . . . an inventive and imaginative winger.

emerged as a dazzling match winner when parading his skills with DWS Amsterdam and attracted Anderlecht's attention because of his versatility that enabled him to play on either wing or in midfield

Smooth and elegant, he has often been mistaken for the great Johan Cruyff as he has a similar slim, wiry build and the same type of inventive mind and movement. He converted four penalties in the 1978 tournament in Argentina and the one he slotted home against Scotland was the one-thousandth goal in World Cup finals. Rensenbrink later flourished his skill on the United States circuit with Portland Timbers.

REP, Johnny (Holland)

His instinct for being in the right place at the right time and a fierce finishing shot made Rep an important cog in the Ajax and Dutch teams of the 1970s. It was his headed goal that clinched a hat-trick of European Cup triumphs for Ajax against Juventus in 1973 and he contributed four goals in the 1974 World Cup finals and another three in 1978. Though lacking the finesse and flair of some of his team-mates, Rep could disturb the tightest defences with his power and drive. He later starred in French football, giving punch to the St Etienne attack after a spell with Bastia.

RIMET, Jules

The Jules Rimet Trophy, won outright by Brazil in 1970, was named after the man who did more than anybody to turn the dream of a World Cup tournament into reality. Rimet, a persuasive, diplomatic Frenchman who shared his countryman Henri Delaunay's vision and organisational flair, was President of the French Football Federation for 30 years from its beginning in 1919. He was the most influential man in world football from 1920 until 1954 while serving as President of FIFA, the game's ruling body. He himself presented the Jules Rimet

JULES RIMET . . . the man who had a dream (pictured being introduced to the Argentinian team before a 1951 international at Wembley).

Trophy to FIFA in 1930. It stood 12 inches high, weighed less than nine pounds and was made of solid gold. It was designed by French sculptor Abel Lafleur. The new FIFA Trophy, designed by an Italian, is 20 inches high, is cast in gold and weighs 11 pounds.

RIVA, Luigi (Italy)

'Gigi' Riva twice recovered from the footballer's nightmare of a broken leg to emerge as one of the most dynamic strikers in Italian football history. He spent most of his headline-hitting career with Cagliari after starting with little Legnano. His goal output turned Cagliari from a second Division club into a power in the Italian First Division and they captured the League championship in 1970.

It was Riva's goal that helped Italy win the 1968 European Nations Cup Final against Yugoslavia and he was the most prominent player in the Italian team that finished runners-up to Brazil in the 1970 World Cup Final. Born at Leggiuno on 7 November 1944, he had a 'golden' left foot that made him one of the wealthiest players of all time. Riva played two matches for Italy in the 1974 World Cup finals.

RIVELINO, Roberto (Brazil)

Whether wide on the left wing or patrolling deep in midfield, Rivelino had the left-foot shooting power and passing accuracy to cause confusion in the most disciplined defences. He was a rival to Gerson for a midfield place in the Brazilian team during the build-up to the 1970 World Cup finals. Manager Mario Zagola solved the team selection problem by picking Rivelino as an orthodox outside-left from where his viciously swerving left-foot shots continually wrong-footed goalkeepers.

After helping Brazil to win the 1970 tournament, the moustachioed, stockily built Rivelino became his country's main midfield motivator in the 1974 and 1978 finals. Born in Sao Paulo on 19 January 1946, he was idolised in Brazil while playing for Corinthians and Fluminense and was later paid a small fortune to take his enormous talent to the playing fields of Saudi Arabia.

RIVERA, Gianni (Italy)

Known as 'The Golden boy' of Italian football, Rivera more than lived up to his tremendous potential when, as a 15-year-old inside-left, he made his first-team debut for Alessandria. Within a year he had joined AC Milan where he became the most gifted forward in the Italian League. The son of a railway worker, Rivera was born on 8 August 1943 and played for Italy in four World Cup final tournaments. His precise passes and imaginative positional play helped steer AC Milan to two European Cup triumphs in the Cup Winners' Cup.

COMMENTS

'Our paths crossed during my brief stay at AC Milan and I knew from my first look at him that he was going to become one of the world's great players. He was beautifully balanced and played an authoritative thinking man's game, even as a teenager. He and football were good for each other. It made him so wealthy that he was able to buy out the AC Milan club President and instal his own man!'

ROUS, Sir Stanley (England)

One of the finest football administrators in the history of the game, Sir Stanley Rous was President of FIFA for 13 years from 1961. He gave a lifetime's service to the game, first as a referee, then as secretary of the Football Association, a job he held for 28 years until taking over as head of FIFA. He

ROBERTO RIVELINO . . . shrugs off a challenge from Italy's Aldo Maldera during the 1978 World Cup finals.

GIANNI RIVERA . . . the 'thinking man's footballer.'

was a schoolmaster before switching to football administration and was also one of England's top referees, reaching a peak when he was in charge of the 1934 FA Cup Final. Born in Mutford, Suffolk, on 25 April 1895, he was knighted for his services to the game in 1949 and was made honorary President of FIFA in 1974.

RUMANIA

Their record in World Cup final tournaments:

1930 Peru (3–1), Uruguay (0–4).

1934 Czechoslovakia (1–2). Eliminated.
1938 Cuba (3–3, replay 1–2). Eliminated.

1970 England (0–1), Czechoslovakia (2–1), Brazil (2–3).

Summary: P 8 W2 D1 L5 F15 A17

RUSSIA

Their record in World Cup final tournaments:

1958 England (2–2), Austria (2–0), Brazil (0–2), England (1–0, play-off), Sweden (0–2, quarter-finals).

1962 Yugoslavia (2–0), Colombia (4–4), Uruguay (2–1), Chile (1–2, quarter-finals).

1966 North Korea (3–0), Italy (1–0), Chile (2–1), Hungary (2–1), West Germany (1–2, semi-final), Portugal (1–2). Finished fourth.

1970 Mexico (0–0), Belgium (4–1), El Salvador (2–0), Uruguay (0–1, quarter-finals).

Summary: P19 W10 D3 L6 F30 A21

Russia did not enter the World Cup until 1958. They withdrew from the tournament in 1974 after refusing to play Chile for political reasons, and defeats by Hungary prevented them qualifying for the 1978 finals. Their current team is rated as good as any in their history.

SANTOS, Djalma (Brazil)

This muscular yet elegant right-back was a cornerstone of Brazil's defence in four World Cup tournaments and collected a winners' medal in 1958 and again in 1962. He was capped 101 times and was renowned for the quickness of his tackling, his superb positional sense and his adventurous attacking play. Born into a poor black family in Sao Paulo in 1929, Santos used soccer as a springboard away from the poverty trap and quickly established himself as an outstanding defender with the Portuguese de Desportos club. He later played for Palmeiras and then, after a brief retirement, Atletico Paranaense, for whom he continued to play into his 40s. He had a long and productive partnership with his unrelated namesake Nilton Santos.

DJALMA SANTOS . . . a cornerstone of Brazil's defence in four World Cup tournaments.

SANTOS, Nilton (Brazil)

His 16 appearances in World Cup final matches are a record for Brazil. In 1962 he became, at 36, the oldest man to collect a World Cup winners' medal and he was still fit and determined enough to win his eighty-fifth cap at the age of 40. He was a skilful and composed left-back who balanced perfectly with his long-time partner Djalma Santos. Both of them were masters of positive overlapping play and used to take turns to make probing runs into the opposition territory.

Born on the Governor's Island near Rio de Janeiro in 1926, Nilton had a long, distinguished career with Botafogo. He was noted for his coolness and command in moments of crisis, a reputation that was dented in the notorious 'Battle of Berne' when he was sent off with Hungarian Josef Bozsik after they had swapped punches in the 1954 World Cup quarter-final. He was a World Cup winner in 1958 and 1962.

SAROSI, Gyorgy (Hungary)

Sarosi played one match in the 1934 World Cup finals and four years later captained the Hungarian team that finished runners-up to Italy in Paris. Most effective at centre-forward, he was also a powerful force as an attacking centre-half. His versatility made him a key member of the Ferencvaros team between the wars and he proved his finishing prowess with five goals in an international match against Czechoslovakia in 1937.

SCARONE, Hector (Uruguay)

His gift for turning half-chances into goals helped Uruguay win the Olympic title in 1924 and 1928 and the World Cup in 1930. He was a fast and clever inside-right who could curl right-footed shots while moving at top speed. Capped 64 times while playing for Nacional, he later played in Europe with Barcelona and Inter-Ambrosia.

SCHIAFFINO, Juan (Uruguay and Italy)

It was his equalising goal that was the turning point in the 1950 World Cup deciding match between Uruguay and Brazil. His ability to make and take goals made him an eye-catching success in the 1950 tournament and his deft skills and incisive finishing were on show again in the 1954 finals, after which AC Milan were moved to buy him from Penarol for £72,000. In his first season in Italy he helped Milan win the League championship and he was capped by Italy and played for them in the 1958 World Cup qualifying tournament. Born in Montevideo on 28 July 1925, he had a deceptively casual stride but could be dynamic in the penalty area and masterly in midfield. He later played for Roma before becoming a manager in Uruguay.

SCHNELLINGER, Karl-Heinz (West Germany)

Though renowned as one of Europe's finest left-backs, Schnellinger made the first of his 17 World Cup final appearances at right-half in the 1958 tournament. Few players can match his World Cup record. He played in one Final (1966), two semi-finals and three quarter-finals between 1962 and 1970, and was also in action in the play-off for third place against France in 1958.

Born in Duren in 1939, Schnellinger began his career with a local club before joining Cologne with whom he won a League championship medal and the 1962 Footballer of the Year award. AS Roma bought him following the 1962 World Cup and after playing for them and Mantova he settled down to a long and successful career with AC Milan. He showed his versatility in the 1970 tournament when he switched to a sweeper role at the back of the defence, a job he later performed for the Milan club. With his blond hair, powerful build and strength in the tackle, Schnellinger was always easy to pick out on a football field.

COMMENTS

'Whenever I think of Schnellinger, my mind always goes back to the 1966 World Cup Final when he was run ragged by Alan Ball. He was given such a run-around that I didn't expect to see him in international football again but he proved his staying power and his all-round ability by emerging as a world-class sweeper in Mexico in 1970.'

SCHOEN, Helmut (West Germany)

A tall, studious inside-left who won 16 international caps, Helmut Schoen switched to coaching after a knee injury forced his premature retirement from playing in 1951. He served as assistant to national team manager Sepp Herberger for eight years, succeeding him in 1964. He led West Germany to the World Cup final in 1966, the semi-finals in 1970 and then to glorious victory in the 1974 Final in Munich. His critics tried to take the glory away from him, claiming that skipper Franz Beckenbauer was the man who dictated the tactics. But this was being less than fair to a man whose courteous manner and quiet dignity won him and West German football many friends.

Born in Dresden in 1915, Schoen was a brilliant tactician who believed in giving his players room for freedom of expresion. But it turned sour for him in his final World Cup tournament in 1978 when the West German team failed to reach their potential after a lot of bickering over tactics and playing personnel. Yet at the end of his 14-year reign, Schoen could look back with pride and satisfaction on a record that more than matched that of his illustrious predecessor Herberger.

SCHULZ, Willi (West Germany)

West Germany have had few more reliable and powerful defenders than Schulz, who was particularly prominent in their 1966 World Cup team when he held the middle of their defence together with his competitive yet constructive play. Born in 1938, he played for Union Gunningfeld, Schalke 04, and SV Hamburg and switched to the centre of defence after starting off as an orthodox right-half. He appeared in the World Cup finals of 1962 and 1970 but it was his performances in the 1966 tournament that earned him his reputation as one of the world's most disciplined and immovable defenders.

SCHWARZENBECK, Georg (West Germany)

Taking over from Willi Schulz as the strong man in the middle of the West German defence, Schwarzenbeck produced a procession of powerful performances that were rewarded with a World Cup winners' medal in 1974. Tall and heavily built, he lacked the finesse of some of the cultured players around him but he was tough and combative and few forwards relished facing him. He was a solid rather than spectacular player and he anchored the defence of the Bayern Munich team that won three successive European Cup Finals in the 1970s. Schwarzenbeck was included in the 1978 West German squad in Argentina but he spent the tournament as a spectator on the substitutes' bench.

GEORG SCHWARZENBECK . . . a strong man at the heart of the West German defence.

SCOTLAND

Their full record in World Cup final tournaments:

1930/34/38 Scotland were not affiliated to FIFA and so did not compete.

1950 The Home championship was used as a qualifying route, with FIFA inviting the first two teams to play in the finals in Brazil. Scotland decided they would only go if they won the championship and so refused to compete after England had pushed them off the top of the table with a 1–0 victory at Hampden Park.

1954 Austria (0–1). Martin, Cunningham, Aird, Docherty, Davidson, Cowie, McKenzie, Fernie, Mochan, Brown, Ormond.
Uruguay (0–7). Unchanged team.

1958 Yugoslavia (1–1). Younger, Caldow, Hewie, Turnbull, Evans, Cowie, Leggat, Murray (1), Mudie, Collins, Imlach.
Paraguay (2–3). Younger, Parker, Caldow, Turnbull, Evans, Cowie, Leggat, Collins (1), Mudie (1), Robertson, Fernie.
France (1–2). Brown, Caldow, Hewie, Turnbull, Evans, Mackay, Collins, Murray, Mudie, Baird (1), Imlach.

1962/66/70 Failed to qualify.

1974 Zaire (2–0). Harvey, Jardine, McGrain, Bremner, Holton, Blackley, Dalglish (Hutchinson), Hay, Lorimer (1), Jordan (1), Law.
Brazil (0–0). Harvey, Jardine, McGrain, Holton, Buchan, Bremner, Hay, Dalglish, Morgan, Jordan, Lorimer.
Yugoslavia (1–1). Unchanged team. Hutchinson substituted for Dalglish. Jordan scored the goal.

Scotland were undefeated but eliminated on goal difference, finishing behind Brazil and Yugoslavia in their group table.

1978 Peru (1–3). Rough, Burns, Kennedy, Forsyth, Buchan, Rioch (Macari), Masson Gemmill, Hartford, Dalglish, Jordan (1), Johnston.
Iran (1–1). Rough, Buchan (Forsyth), Jardine, Burns, Donachie, Macari, Gemmill, Hartford, Jordan, Dalglish (Harper), Robertson. They scored through an own goal by Eskandarian.
Holland (3–2). Rough, Donachie, Buchan, Kennedy, Forsyth, Rioch, Hartford, Gemmill (2, 1 pen), Souness, Dalglish (1), Jordan.

Summary: P11 W2 D4 L5 F12 A21

UWE SEELER . . . 'played as if he had springs in his legs.'

SEELER, Uwe (West Germany)

Nobody has played more matches in World Cup final tournaments than Seeler, who between 1958 and 1970 appeared in 21 games for West Germany. He skippered the West German team that finished runners-up to England in 1966 and was also an influential player for the Germans in 1958, 1962 and 1970. Though short and stocky, he was an acrobatic centre-forward who could outjump even the tallest defenders to score with flying headers. He was courageous and fought off several injury handicaps to remain a power in international football over a span of 72 matches.

The son of a top-flight player, he was born in Hamburg in 1936 and served SV Hamburg as a prolific goal scorer for twenty years. He was leading marksman in the West German league on five occasions and played his first match for West Germany at the age of 17. His World Cup career seemed over after he had inspired West Germany to the runners-up place in 1966 but he made one of his comebacks to the international arena in 1970 and, concentrating on an auxiliary attacking role, gave Gerd Muller sufficient support to lift the Germans into third position in the tournament.

COMMENTS

'Seeler was a marvellous competitor who played as if he had springs in his legs. He was quick, alert and had an instinctive positional sense that meant he was always getting into areas where he could cause most trouble to defences. Perhaps his greatest gift was his ability to inspire the players around him with his great industry. He always seemed to grow six inches the moment he pulled on an international shirt.'

SKOGLUND, Nacka (Sweden)

Starting and finishing his career in his native Stockholm, Skoglund had eight years with Inter-Milan in between, during which he established himself as one of Europe's most creative forwards. A natural left-footed player, he featured with Sweden in the 1950 World Cup as an inside-left and helped them eliminate Italy on the way to a remarkable third place in the tournament. He then teamed up with Hungary's Stefan Nyers in the Inter-Milan attack and together they steered the Italians to two League championship triumphs

As he got older, Skoglund decided he would be more effective playing wide on the left wing where his clever dribbling, accurate passing and deadly left-foot shooting made him a menace to defences. His wing work played an important part in motivating the Swedish team that finished runners-up to Brazil in the 1958 Final. By then Skoglund was 30 and after a brief spell with Palermo he returned to Sweden for the final shots of his distinguished career.

SOUTH KOREA

South Korea have an unhappy place in the World Cup record books as the team with the worst defensive summary. The only time they qualified for the finals was in 1954 and their first match was against Hungary, then at the peak of their power. The Koreans were hammered 9–0. They then went down 7–0 against Turkey before taking their battered pride back to Asia. It was 12 years before their neighbours and bitter rivals, North Korea, restored respectability to the football-mad area of Asia. *(See North Korea.)*

SPAIN

Their full record in World Cup final tournaments:

1934 Brazil (3–1), Italy (1–1, replay 0–1).
1950 USA (3–1), Chile (2–0), England (1–0), Uruguay (2–2), Brazil (1–6), Sweden (1–3). Finished fourth.

1962 Czechoslovakia (0–1), Mexico (1–0), Brazil (1–2).

1966 Argentina (1–2), Switzerland (2–1), West Germany (1–2).

31978 Austria (1–2), Brazil (0–0), Sweden (1–0).

Summary: P18 W7 L8 F22 A25

STABILE, Guillermo (Argentina)

Nicknamed '*El Infiltrado*' because of his ability to infiltrate the tightest defence, Stabile made a sensational World Cup debut in the 1930 tournament. He was summoned into the Argentina attack for the second match against Mexico in place of skipper Manuel Ferreira, who had to miss the game because of a university examination. Stabile scored a hat-trick in Argentina's 6–3 victory and went on to collect another five goals including a hotly disputed one in the Final which Uruguay argued was offside. He later became a successful club manager before taking over as team manager of the Argentine national team that he had served so well as a player.

NOBBY STILES . . . the 'Toothless Tiger.' ▶

STILES, Nobby (England)

A warrior of a footballer, Nobby Stiles was totally committed to every match he played in and was rarely popular with the opposition, who felt the fierce force of his tigerish challenges. He was the midfield motivator for the England team that won the 1966 World Cup and for the Manchester United side that won the European Cup in 1968. Though only small and slight, Stiles strode the pitch like a giant and was frightened of no situation or reputation. He was a master at winning the ball with well-timed interceptions and biting tackles. It was thanks largely to his dynamic approach to every game that the teams he played with used to enjoy so much possession. He would win the ball and then pass it to players with more finesse to capitalise on his work.

Born in Manchester on 18 May 1942, Stiles wore contact lenses while playing but he always had a good eye for turning defence into attack with well-delivered passes. He later played for Middlesbrough and Preston before having a spell as Preston manager in succession to his old Manchester United and England team-mate Bobby Charlton.

COMMENTS

'Nobby was a far more skilful and subtle player than most people realised. He was an aggressive, competitive blighter who would never concede an inch to the opposition but there was also a lot of constructive work in his play. He was a marvellous bloke to have on your side and would lift his team-mates by the force of his personality. Yet funnily enough, off the pitch Nobby was the quietest person you could meet. He was a lamb until he pulled on a football shirt and then he became a lion. What a character!'

SUBSTITUTES

Substitutes were allowed in the World Cup finals for the first time in 1970. The first player to come on from the substitutes' bench was Russian forward Puzach, who replaced team-mate Serebrianikov at half-time in the opening match of the tournament against host country Mexico. Gianni Rivera came on as a substitute for Italy in four matches in the 1970 tournament without playing a complete game. This included coming into the World Cup Final against Brazil with only six minutes to go. Just nine minutes earlier Juliano had become the first substitute used in a World Cup Final when he replaced injured Italian team-mate Bertini.

SUURBIER, Wim (Holland)

An adventurous full-back with a winger's speed and skill, Suurbier brought flair to the Dutch defence. He collected a runners-up medal in 1974 and came on as a substitute in the 1978 final against Argentina. Born on 16 January 1945, he joined Ajax from DWS Amsterdam and played at left-back in the team that won the European Cup and on the right flank when Ajax completed the hat-trick in 1972 and 1973. He later moved to West Germany with Schalke 04.

SWEDEN

Their full record in World Cup final tournaments:

1934 Argentina (3–2), Germany (1–2). Eliminated.

1938 Cuba (8–0), Hungary (1–5), Brazil (2–4). Finished fourth.

1950 Italy (3–2), Paraguay (2–2), Brazil (1–7), Uruguay (2–3), Spain (3–1). Finished third.

1958 Mexico (3–0), Hungary (2–1), Wales (0–0), Russia (2–0), West Germany (3–1), Brazil (2–5, final). Runners-up.

1970 Italy (0–1), Israel (1–1), Uruguay (1–0).

1974 Bulgaria (0–0), Holland (0–0), Uruguay (3–0), Poland (0–1), West Germany (2–4), Yugoslavia (2–1).

1978 Brazil (1–1), Austria (0–1), Spain (0–1).

Summary: P28 W10 D6 L8 F34 A28

SWITZERLAND

Their full record in World Cup final tournaments:

1934 Holland (3–2), Czechoslovakia (2–3). Eliminated.

1938 Germany (1–1, replay 4–2), Hungary (0–2).

1950 Yugoslavia (0–3), Brazil (2–2), Mexico (2–1).

1954 England (0–2), Italy (2–1, play-off 4–1), Austria (5–7, quarter-finals).

1962 Chile (1–3), West Germany (1–2), Italy (0–3).

1966 West Germany (0–5), Spain (1–2), Argentina (0–2).

Summary: P18 W5 D2 L11 F28 A44

TELEVISION

The first 'live' television coverage of the World Cup was in Switzerland in 1954. There was a European audience estimated at several hundred thousand. By

1978 the world-wide audience was closer to 600 million. The demands and dictates of television brought severe criticism during the 1970 tournament in the thin air of Mexico when teams had to go out in the midday sun to suit television programme deadlines.

TOSTAO, Eduard Concalves de Andrade (Brazil)

It was something of a miracle that Tostao was able to flourish his great talent in the Brazilian attack in the 1970 World Cup finals. In the previous year he had undergone two delicate eye operations for a detached retina. A ball had struck him in the eye during a training session and the first fears were that he would never play football again. But the skill of an American surgeon coupled with Tostao's courage and determination meant he was able to take his place as leader of Brazil's stunning forward-line. He was a key member because it was his ability to lay the ball off and take up intelligent positions that knitted the attack together.

Born in 1947, he was just 19 when he made his World Cup debut in 1966. Four years later, after studying at university in Belo Horizonte, he had matured and developed into a magnificent all-round player and his imaginative performances with Cruziero in the Brazilian League made him a must to link up with Jairzinho, Gerson, Pele and Rivelino in one of the greatest of all World Cup attack forces.

TUNISIA

Unrated Tunisia provided the first sensation of the 1978 World Cup finals when they came from a goal behind against Mexico to win 3–1. The North Africans had qualified from a group in which they were held to a draw by Nigeria and beaten by Egypt and it was widely forecast that they would be way out of their depth in the finals. But they stunned Mexico with their smooth team play and there were several individual players whose skills were well suited to the World Cup stage.

They proved their victory against Mexico was no fluke when they gave the powerful Polish team a hard struggle before going down to a 1–0 defeat. In their last World Cup appearance the Tunisians played a determined defensive game that was rewarded with a stunning goalless draw against defending world champions West Germany. They were out of the tournament but had won many friends and admirers with the spirit and style of their challenge.

TURKEY

Turkey had mixed fortunes in their one appearance in the World Cup finals in 1954. They were beaten 4–1 by eventual champions West Germany but buried South Korea under an avalanche of seven goals to qualify for a play-off against West Germany. A hat-trick from Max Morlock helped the Germans sweep to a 7–2 victory. Turkey also qualified for the 1950 finals but withdrew after beating Syria 7–0.

UNITED STATES OF AMERICA

Their full record in World Cup final tournaments:

1930 Belgium (3–0), Paraguay (3–0), Argentina (1–6, semi-finals).

1934 Italy (1–7). Eliminated.

1950 Spain (1–3), England (1–0), Chile (2–5).

The United States team pulled off a victory over England that sent shock waves through the world of football. England, the Old Masters who had given football to the world, were among the favourites for the tournament and no wonder with a squad that included all-time heroes like Stanley Matthews, Tom Finney, Wilf Mannion, Stan Mortensen and Billy Wright. England elected to rest the legendary Matthews for what was expected to be a victory stroll against the Americans. Soccer was still an infant sport in the States and the World Cup, even the win against England, was given little coverage by the media. Everywhere else in the football world England's defeat made front-page news. It was wrongly and unfairly reported at the time that the United States players had come *en masse* from Ellis Island and did not include a single American-born member. In fact all but three of their team were United States citizens by birth. The three 'imports' were Joe Maca of Belgium, Ed McIllvenny of Scotland and goal-scorer Larry ('Joe' to his team-mates) Gaetjens of Haiti.

For the record, this was the United States team that provided English football with the most embarrassing day in its history: Borghi, Keough, Maca, McIllvenny (capt), Colombo, Bahr, Wallace, Pariani, Gaetjens, E. Souza, J. Souza. England's line-up: Williams, Ramsey, Aston, Wright (capt), Hughes, Dickinson, Finney, Mortensen, Bentley, Mannion, Mullen.

Just 16 days earlier, with Matthews in the line-up, England had struggled to a 1–0 victory over the United States in an unofficial international match in New York. But even this close encounter provided no warning of the shock waiting for England in Belo Horizonte – 'Beautiful Horizon'!

CBD

◀ **TOSTAO . . . the man who pulled the Brazilian attack together.**

URUGUAY

Their full record in World Cup final tournaments:

1930 Peru (1–0), Romania (4–0), Yugoslavia (6–1), Argentina (4–2, final). Champions.

1934/38 Did not compete.

1950 Bolivia (8–0), Spain (2–2), Sweden (3–2), Brazil (2–1, final). Champions.

1954 Czechoslovakia (2–0), Scotland (7–0), England (4–2), Hungary (2–4, semi-final), Austria (1–3). Finished fourth.

1958 Failed to qualify (eliminated by Paraguay).

1962 Colombia (2–1), Yugoslavia (1–3), Russia (1–2).

1966 England (0–0), France (2–1), Mexico (0–0), West Germany (0–4, quarter-finals).

1970 Israel (2–0), Italy (0–0), Sweden (0–1), Russia (1–0), Brazil (1–3, semi-final), West Germany (0–1). Finished fourth.

1974 Holland (0–2), Bulgaria (1–1), Sweden (0–3).

Summary: P29 W14 D5 L10 F57 A39

In terms of population, Uruguay have the best of all World Cup records. They have only just over three million people living in Uruguay but have managed to produce two World Cup-winning teams. Along with Italy (1938) and Brazil (1970), their 1930 side was the only team to have won every game in a final series. They did not lose a single match in World Cup competition from the first tournament in 1930 until their semi-final defeat by Hungary in 1954, a match that was rated one of the classic contests in World Cup history.

THE FIRST HAND-OVER . . . Uruguay Football Association President Dr Paul Jude (right) receives the World Cup from Jules Rimet after the 1930 Final against Argentina.

RENE VAN DER KERKHOF . . . a twin-propelled striker for Holland.

VAN DER KERKHOF, Rene and Willy (Holland)

The Van der Kerkhof brothers were born in Helmond, Holland, on 16 September 1951. They are spitting-image identical twins and share the same skills, technique and temperament on the football field. Reiner (Rene) and Wilhelmus (Willy) started in football together for the junior team of FC Mulo of Helmond, at the age of eight. Their dual potential was quickly spotted by Twente Enschede who signed them as professionals at 18. Three years later they moved to PSV Eindhoven and soon after made their international debuts together against Austria.

Both were in the 1974 Dutch World Cup squad, Rene coming on in the Final as substitute for injured Robbie Rensenbrink. Four years later, both played in the 1978 Final against Argentina. Willy is a powerful and creative midfield player, while Rene is a quick, driving front-line player who likes to attack down the right flank.

VAN HANEGEM, Wim (Holland)

With a left foot that can hook fish, Wim van Hanegem was the key midfield player for the Dutch team that finished runners-up to West Germany in the 1974 World Cup Final. Born on 20 February 1944 (the day that Jimmy Greaves was celebrating his fourth birthday!), van Hanegem proved himself a world-class schemer when he joined Feyenoord from their Rotterdam neighbours Xerces. It was his calm, unhurried and deadly accurate work in midfield that guided Feyenoord to victory over Celtic in the 1970 European Cup Final. Holland were counting on him to help mount their 1978 World Cup challenge but he explained tearfully on television that he was neither mentally nor physically prepared for another final series.

VARELA, Obdulio (Uruguay)

Varela's inspiring leadership was an important factor in Uruguay's 1950 World Cup triumph. Born in 1915, he became the oldest man to captain a World Cup-winning team. But he still was not finished and was back in World Cup action again four years later in Switzerland. His international career spanned 15 years, starting with an explosive debut against Brazil in 1940 when he scored a hat-trick from the inside-left position. He later developed into an attacking centre-half, his large, powerful frame making him an effective force in both penalty areas. Varela was one of seven Penarol players in the Uruguayan team that mastered Brazil in the deciding match in the 1950 tournament.

VAVA, Evaldo Izidio Neto (Brazil)

Vava is the only player to have scored goals in consecutive World Cup Finals. He notched two for Brazil against Sweden in 1958 and the third goal against Czechoslovakia in the 1962 Final. A slim, thrusting player, Vava combined the brave, aggressive qualities of British-style centre-forwards with the gazelle-like grace of Brazilian ball artists.

Born in Recife in 1934, he first played for a small local club before joining Rio-based Vasco da Gama. He was 17 when he played for Brazil in the 1952 Olympics and he went to the 1958 World Cup as understudy to Jose Altafini who later became a star of Italian football. Altafini's attitude did not please Brazilian coach Vicente Feola and he decided instead to play Vava who, in the second half of the tournament, proved a perfect partner for the young Pele. Vava later joined Atletico Madrid and after two successful years in Spain he returned to Brazil to play for Palmeiras in Sao Paulo. He wound down his career in the Mexican League.

COMMENTS

'Vava was a dream of a centre-forward who was not particularly big but seemed to grow several inches the moment he motored into the penalty area. He was a master at playing the ball off with exactly the right amount of weight and he was a deadly finisher whether receiving the ball to his head or feet.'

VOGTS, Bertie (West Germany)

It was his disciplined marking of Johan Cruyff that played a vital part in West Germany's victory over Holland in the 1974 World Cup Final. Born on 20 December 1946, Vogts developed his defensive technique with his local club, VfR Buttgen, before joining Borussia Moenchengladbach in 1965. Two-footed and quick, he brought an adventurous spirit to his right-back play and his enthusiastic overlapping runs were an important attacking weapon for his club and country. He succeeded Franz Beckenbauer as West Germany's captain and led the 1978 World Cup defence in Argentina.

VORONIN, Valeri (Russia)

A strong and skilful midfield player, Voronin was the main driving force for the Russian team that reached the 1962 World Cup quarter-finals and the semi-final in 1966. Born in 1939, he had an outstanding career with Moscow Torpedo and then Spartak until a late-night car crash wrecked his sporting life. He was dubbed as a playboy and was publicly pilloried by clubmates who claimed he was setting a bad example for young footballers. It was a sad end to what had been a distinguished career that included more than 50 international appearances.

WALES

Wales took a curious route to their one appearance in the World Cup finals in 1958. They were eliminated in their qualifying group after finishing second to Czechoslovakia but they got an unexpected second chance when Israel's opponents all withdrew for political reasons. FIFA held a draw and it was Wales who came out of the hat as the country to face Israel for the right to a place in the finals. Wales duly won and took their place in a tough group in Sweden in which their opponents were Sweden, Hungary and Mexico. Inspired by the power and skill of John Charles, the creative force of Ivor Allchurch, the driving midfield play of Dave Bowen, the dash of young Cliffie Jones and the safe hands of goalkeeper Jack Kelsey, Wales equipped themselves well and reached the quarter-finals after beating Hungary in a play-off. They were finally eliminated by Brazil, going down to a 1–0 defeat and a first World Cup goal scored by a youngster called Pele.
The Welsh line-ups in the 1958 finals:

Hungary (1–1). Kelsey, Williams, Hopkins, Sullivan, M. Charles, Bowen, Webster, Medwin, J. Charles (1), Allchurch, Jones.

Mexico (1–1). Same team, apart from Baker for Sullivan. Scorer: Allchurch.

Sweden (0–0). Kelsey, Williams, Hopkins, Sullivan, M. Charles, Bowen, Vernon, Hewitt, J. Charles, Allchurch, Jones.

◀ JOHN CHARLES . . . powerful in both penalty areas for Wales.

Hungary (2–1, play-off). Same team, apart from Medwin for Vernon. Scorers: Allchurch and Medwin.

Brazil (0–1, quarter-final). Kelsey, Williams, Hopkins, Sullivan, M. Charles, Bowen, Medwin, Hewitt, Webster, Allchurch, Jones.

In the quarter-final, Colin Webster replaced John Charles who was injured by some brutal Hungarian tackling in the group play-off.

WALTER, Fritz (West Germany)

Captain of the 1954 World Cup winners, Walter was the midfield marshall for a West German team that stunned hot-favourites Hungary to defeat in the Final in Switzerland. He was then 33 and carried on playing in international football for another four years, leading West Germany in the 1958 finals in Sweden where his midfield authority and controlled passing was again a feature of the tournament as it had been in 1954.

Born in Kaiserlautern in 1921, Walter was a former paratrooper who refused to fly again after the Second World War because of a nightmare experience when a close friend was killed beside him during an air-raid. He and his brother Otmar were idolised in Kaiserlautern where they developed into a great tandem team, Otmar doing the shooting and Fritz the scheming. Fritz had been a striker early in his career but decided to drop back into midfield and provide passes for his brother.

They played together in the 1954 Final but Otmar had dropped out of the international scene by the time of the 1958 finals. Fritz scored 33 goals in 61 appearances for West Germany. In the 1954 semi-final he and Otmar scored two goals each in the 6–1 hammering of Austria.

Turkey's defenders give a new meaning to the saying 'backs to the wall' as Fritz Walter drives a free-kick towards goal during the 1954 World Cup finals.

WEST GERMANY

(See also Germany)

Their full record in World Cup final tournaments:

1954 Turkey (4–1), Hungary (3–8), Turkey (7–2, play-off), Yugoslavia (2–0), Austria (6–1), Hungary 3–2, final). Champions.

1958 Argentina (3–1), Czechoslovakia (2–2), Northern Ireland (2–2), Yugoslavia (1–0), Sweden (1–3, semi-final), France (3–6). Finished fourth.

1962 Italy (0–0), Switzerland (2–1), Chile (2–0), Yugoslavia (0–1, quarter-final).

1966 Switzerland (5–0), Argentina (0–0), Spain (2–1), Uruguay (4–0), Russia (2–1), England (2–4, final). Runners-up.

1970 Morocco (2–1), Bulgaria (5–2), Peru (3–1), England (3–2), Italy (3–4, semi-final), Uruguay (1–0). Finished third.

1974 Chile (1–0), Australia (3–0), East Germany (0–1), Yugoslavia (2–0), Sweden (4–2), Poland (1–0), Holland (2–1, final). Champions.

1978 Poland (0–0), Mexico (6–0), Tunisia (0–0), Italy (0–0), Holland (2–2), Austria (2–3).

Summary: P41 W25 D8 L8 F96 A55

Only Brazil have a better World Cup success record. West Germany have never failed to reach the quarter-finals or the equivalent round in any year they competed. They have been champions twice, runners-up once and have been third and fourth. They were also third in 1934 before Germany was split into East and West.

WILSON, Ray (England)

Born in Shirebrook, Yorkshire, on 17 December 1934, Ramon (Ray) Wilson was 25 before he made his England debut. He went on to make 63 international appearances in eight years, firmly establishing himself as one of the world's outstanding left-backs. It was Bill ('The Liverpool Legend') Shankly who, while manager of Huddersfield, switched Wilson to full-back after he had struggled to make any sort of impact as a wing-half. It was a master move and he quickly developed into one of the most accomplished defenders in the League, tight and disciplined with his marking and tackling and immaculate with his distribution.

He moved from Huddersfield to Everton in 1965 and collected an FA Cup winners' medal just a few weeks before helping England win the 1966 World Cup at Wembley. A succession of injuries handicapped him and he had a short spell at Oldham, then as a coach at Bradford city, before retiring to concentrate on a starkly different life as a funeral director.

RAY WILSON . . . 'a thoroughbred of a full-back.'

COMMENTS

'One of my all-time favourite players, Ray was a thoroughbred of a full-back who had the creative skill of an inside-forward and tigerish determination that meant he refused to be beaten. He was terrific for team spirit because of his pleasant personality and his partnerships with first Jimmy Armfield and then George Cohen were as perfect as any I've seen in a defence. It's difficult to imagine him in his role as an undertaker because his sense of humour meant he always had anybody in his company laughing at his sharp wit. A smashing bloke and a smashing player.'

BILLY WRIGHT . . . 'he lit a torch.' ▶

WINTERBOTTOM, Sir Walter (England)

As team manager and the FA's chief coach, Walter Winterbottom led England through four World Cup campaigns but without any startling success. He was England mastermind for the World Cup finals of 1950, 1954, 1958 and 1962 until giving way to Alf Ramsey. Born in Lancashire in 1913, he was a former schoolmaster who briefly played professional football with Manchester United. His greatest contribution to English football was the setting up of a coaching network that continues to flourish. He became General Secretary of the Central Council of Physical Recreation in 1963 and was knighted for his services to sport. England's record in World Cup finals under Winterbottom's guidance was: P14, W3, D5, L6, F19, A21

COMMENTS

'Walter was a thoroughly nice man who was a little too keen on football theory for my personal taste. He might have been more successful as England's manager had he not been stifled by the need to work in harness with a team of selectors who filled few people with confidence. His deep knowledge of sports administration was lost to football when the FA blindly refused to appoint him Secretary of their Association when Sir Stanley Rous became President of FIFA. He still had so much to give to a game he had served so well since taking over the coaching reins at the FA back in 1946.'

WRIGHT, Billy (England)

This stalwart defender captained England in the World Cup finals of 1950, 1954 and 1958. He was a magnificent field marshal, captaining Wolves to a succession of memorable triumphs in the 1950s and leading England 90 times while winning a then record 105 international caps. Born at Ironbridge, Shropshire, on 6 February 1924, he started his career as an inside-forward before developing into a driving right-half. He switched to centre-half in an emergency for the 1954 World Cup finals and went on to establish himself as one of England's greatest ever central defenders. Greatly respected by team-mates and opponents alike, he had a spell as England under-23 and Arsenal manager at the close of his distinguished career before becoming a television executive.

COMMENTS

'Billy was one of my idols when I was a schoolboy with dreams of becoming a professional footballer and it was a pleasure to play with and against him at the back-end of his fabulous career. England has never had a greater or more loyal servant and his exploits with the wonderful Wolves side of the 1950s lit a torch for many young players, myself included. He is now my boss at Central Television in the Midlands where he is the same affable, approachable and likeable personality he always used to be as a player.'

YASHIN, Lev (Russia)

One of the legendary figures of football, Yashin was Russia's commanding last line of defence in 74 international matches during which he became world-renowned for his agility and astonishing reflex saves. Born in Moscow in 1929, he played throughout his career for Moscow Dynamo. His loyalty to the club was rewarded in 1971 when a capacity 100,000 crowd packed the Lenin Stadium to see Yashin in his farewell match, skippering a Moscow Dynamo team against a Rest of the World side captained by Bobby Charlton.

Standing 6ft 2in and always dressed in black, he was an imposing figure on the goal-line, and his expert positioning and seeming telescopic reach meant forwards were rarely given more than a glimpse at their target. He played for Russia in the World Cup finals of 1958, 1962 and 1966, and travelled to Mexico in 1970 as a distinguished reserve.

COMMENTS

'He is the only goalkeeper I ever faced who could possibly rival Gordon Banks and Pat Jennings for the title of the world's Number One 'keeper. I well remember his performance for the Rest of the World against England in the centenary match at Wembley in 1963. But for his mind-boggling saves I would have had four goals in the first half. I don't say that to boast about my performance but to illustrate what a genius of a goalkeeper he was. Yashin was also a thoroughly sporting and warm opponent who was a marvellous ambassador for his country.'

LEV YASHIN . . . commanding last line of defence.

ZAGALO, Mario Jorge Lobo (Brazil)

This clever, calculating left-winger was with the Brazilian teams that won the World Cup in 1958 and 1962 and he carried his tactician's mind into management, masterminding his country's World Cup triumph in Mexico in 1970. Born in 1931 of Italian extraction, Zagalo started his professional career with Flamengo after starring as an amateur with Maguari and FC America. He was never an orthodox outside-left, preferring to patrol in mid-field and make undetected runs from deep postions. His accurate crosses produced dozens of goals and he was also a dangerous finisher when cutting in at the end of zig-zagging runs that confused a procession of full-backs.

Botafogo bought him after the 1962 World Cup triumph but he was never quite the same force after breaking a leg playing against his old Flamengo club. An exceptional organiser, he took over as manager of Brazilian champions Fluminense after being inconsiderately sacked as Brazil manager. He later had a spell in charge of Vasco da Gama.

MARIO ZAGALO . . . an organiser on and off the pitch.

YUGOSLAVIA

Their full record in World Cup final tournaments:

1930 Brazil (2–1), Bolivia (4–0), Uruguay (1–6, semi-final).

1950 Switzerland (3–0), Mexico (4–1), Brazil (0–2).

1954 France (1–0), Brazil (1–1), West Germany (0–2).

1958 Scotland (1–1), France (3–2), Paraguay (3–3), West Germany (0–1, quarter-final).

1962 Russia (0–2), Uruguay (3–1), Colombia (5–0), West Germany (1–0), Czechoslovakia (1–3, semi-final), Chile (0–1). Finished fourth.

1974 Brazil (0–0), Zaire (9–0), Scotland (1–1), West Germany (0–2), Poland (1–2), Sweden (1–2).

Summary: P25 W10 D5 L10 F45 A34

DINO ZOFF (Italy) . . . being beaten for once (by a Kevin Keegan header at Wembley in 1977).

ZAIRE

Zaire battled bravely in their only appearance in the World Cup finals but they were always struggling in the 1974 tournament, conceding 14 goals and not having the satisfaction of scoring a single goal themselves. They conceded two goals against Scotland, nine against Yugoslavia and three against Brazil. Like Morocco, their predeccors as winners of the 1970 African group, Zaire were coached by former Yugoslav international goalkeeper Vidinic. Zaire had some talented individual players but their tactical awareness was at times novice-like.

ZITO, Jose Eli Mirana (Brazil)

A gifted all purpose player, Zito brought a new dimension to Brazil's midfield when he took over from Dino in the 1958 World Cup finals. He provided the perfect balance to Didi in Brazil's 4–2–4 formation, anchoring the team with his sound tackling and also making a creative contribution with passes that were always accurate and imaginative. Born in Roseira in 1933, Zito started his career with his local club before joining Taubate and then linking up with Pele at Santos. He helped Brazil retain the World Cup in 1962 and came to England for the 1966 finals but injury kept him on the sidelines.

ZIZINHO, Tomas Soares Da Silva (Brazil)

Zizinho teamed up with Ademir and Jair in the magnificent Brazilian inside-forward trio of the immediate post-war years and collected a runners-up medal in the 1950 World Cup finals. He was all elegance and style, and had a casual, relaxed approach to the game that could be misinterpreted as disinterest. Many defenders made the mistake of thinking he was less than totally committed to a match and suddenly found themselves tackling his shadow as he went past them in an explosion of action.

Born in Niteroi in 1921, he had a distinguished international career that lasted until he was 35. He first played with his local club Carioca but it was with Rio clubs Flamengo and Bangu that he established himself as one of the world's most skilled forwards.

ZOFF, Dino (Italy)

Following the forced retirement of Gordon Banks, Zoff challenged Sepp Maier for the title of 'the world's greatest goalkeeper'. When Haiti scored against Italy in the 1974 World Cup finals, it was the first time Zoff had been beaten in 1,143 minutes of international football.

Born in Mariano del Friuli on 28 February 1942, he played for Udinese, Mantova and Naples before joining Juventus in 1972. He was Italy's last line of defence when they won the Nations Cup in 1968 and then lost his place to Albertosi for the 1970 finals in Mexico. But he was back in favour for the 1974 finals and captained the 1978 World Cup team in Argentina. Tall, agile and with excellent positional sense and astonishing reflexes, Zoff collected a runners-up medal with Juventus in the 1973 European Cup Final.

The 1982 Finals

SPAIN

See pages 140-143 for World Cup diary and results chart.

Introduction

The 1982 World Cup Finals in Spain will have a completely new formula, with the number of finalists raised for the first time to twenty four. There will be 52 matches played in 29 days and staged in 14 cities across Spain culminating with the Final in Madrid on 11 July.

A total of 109 countries entered the 1982 World Cup and there were 305 qualifying matches to decide the twenty four finalists. Six countries were selected to be seeded for the group matches in Spain: hosts *Spain*, World Cup holders *Argentina* and former champions *Italy*, *West Germany*, *England* and *Brazil*. There was considerable controversy as to England's merit as seeds but official protests from Belgium and France were dismissed by FIFA, football's world-governing body.

The twenty four qualifiers will play three matches each in the first phase of the tournament between 13 June and 25 June. The top two teams in the six qualifying groups will go forward to the second round and will be drawn into four groups of three teams each. Each team will play against each other on a mini-league basis and the four teams who top their groups on points or goal difference will qualify for the semi-finals.

Jimmy Greaves has studied the strengths and weaknesses of each of the twenty four qualifiers and in this section gives his expert analysis of the The Contenders for the championship . . .

Group 1

ITALY

Colours: Blue shirts/white shorts
Manager: Enzo Bearzot
Qualifying results: Luxemburg (A) 2–0, (H) 1–0; Denmark (H) 2–0, (A) 1–3; Greece (A) 2–0, (H) 1–1; Yugoslavia (H) 2–0, (A) 1–1.
Possible team: Zoff – Gentile, Collovati, Scirea, Cabrini, – Marini, Tardelli, Antognoni – Conti, Rossi, Bettega.

The Italian team will be similar, in style and personnel, to the side that finished fourth in the 1978 finals. Much depends on whether team manager Enzo Bearzot decides to gamble on playing Paolo Rossi. Perhaps *gamble* is the operative word. Rossi has collected rust while serving a suspension for alleged involvement in a betting-and-bribes scandal that rocked Italian football to its foundations. Graziani would be the most likely standby for Rossi if the lay-off has in any way anchored his pace and blunted his skills. There is also doubt about key midfield marshal Giancarlo Antognoni who was put out of action by a fractured skull. I would expect Dossena to deputise which would make the Italian midfield less effective.

Italy will again be relying on a strong Juventus influence and look powerful enough on paper to at least be good enough to reach the semi-final stages. Italy, like England, have a history of occasional World Cup calamities and their players still turn white when they recall the 1966 defeat by North Korea and the tomato bombardment that greeted the team on their return home. But I am confident they will come out on top of Group 1 where Poland and Peru will perhaps give them problems, with Cameroon there to make the numbers up. Italy's opening match against Poland will, to say the least, be fascinating. After their last meeting in World Cup combat in Stuttgart in 1974, the Poles alleged that some Italian players tried to bribe them during the match. The Italians won't need to resort to those measures in Spain.

Rating (out of ten): 8*********

GIANCARLO ANTOGNONI . . . Italy's influential midfield schemer whose World Cup place was put in doubt by a fractured skull. He's pictured here menacing the Brazilian defence during the 1978 World Cup finals.

Group 1

POLAND

Colours: White shirts/red shorts
Manager: Antonio Piechniczek
Qualifying results: Malta (A) 2–0, (H) 6–0; East Germany (H) 1–0, (A) 3–2.
Possible team: Mowlik – Dziuba, Zmuda, Janas, Jalocha – Matysik, Majewski, Boniek – Lato, Szarmach, Smolarek.

In the last decade, Poland has emerged as one of the most powerful football nations in the world but who knows what psychological effect the political events of the last year have had on their players? The Poles have been a pleasure to watch in the last two World Cup tournaments and their two star strikers, Lato and Szarmach, are still going strong. For spectators, there will not be the pleasing sight of goalkeeper Jan Tomaszewski performing eccentric but effective tricks at the back of the defence. The player Brian Clough labelled 'a clown' has left the international soccer circus after winning 65 caps and the job of keeping out the shots is now in the capable hands of Mowlik, a less adventurous but more reliable last line of defence.

It will be interesting to see the role adopted by Grzegorz Lato, who in recent matches has been operating in a dual role of schemer and support striker. He is an exciting match-winning type of player wherever he decides to position himself and any team wanting to beat Poland will first of all have to shackle Lato. The Polish defence will again be under the command of Wladyslaw Zmuda, who remains one of the most authoritative and skilful central defenders in Europe. Only a fool would dismiss Poland, particularly after their two convincing victories over East Germany in the qualifying matches. Their players will be looking to lift the gloom following all the headline-hitting disasters that have paralysed Poland in recent months. I hope they perform well because it would be the best possible morale booster for their shackled countrymen at home.

Rating: 7*****

Peruvian goalkeeper Quiroga halts a Polish raid during the 1978 Finals in Argentina.

Group 1

PERU

Colours: All white.
Manager: Tim (Elba de Padua Lima)
Qualifying results: Colombia (A) 1–1, (H) 2–0; Uruguay (A) 2–1, (H) 0–0.
Possible team: Quiroga – Duarte, Diaz, Chumpitaz, Rojas – Velasquez, Cueto, Uribe – Barbadillo, Cubillas, La Rosa.

It was Peru who underlined the uncertainties of football in the qualifying rounds by eliminating Uruguay, among the favourites for the championship following their victory in the Gold Cup. They have a shrewd tactician guiding them in 71-year-old Brazilian Tim, who has been carefully plotting Peru's World Cup challenge with typical Brazilian thoroughness. But he has been handicapped by having at least half his team travelling the world as soccer mercenaries. Many of his squad are now into the veteran stage and if the gifted but ageing Cubillas does not make it for the finals, then it is likely that the equally explosive Oblitas will take over one of the main striking roles. The chances of unconventional goalkeeper Ramon Quiroga taking his place in defence were complicated by his 60-day suspension (without pay) after being sent off for allegedly suggesting that the referee of his club match was from a single-parent family. If he were absent, it would make the finals less colourful and reduce Peru's chances of surviving to the late stages.

The Peruvians are completely unpredictable and can take any defence in the world apart when in possession. But they are less than dependable under pressure and there has to be question marks about their temperament when things are not going their way. Their vanquishing of Uruguay makes them the dark horses of the tournament. I shall be surprised if they survive the first group of matches but I know from long experience that with the Peruvians anything and everything is possible.

Rating: 6*******

RAMON QUIROGA . . . trouble with a referee.

Group 1

CAMEROON

Colours: Green shirts/red shorts
Manager: Branko Zutic
Qualifying results: Malawi (H) 3–0, (A) 1–1; Zimbabwe (H) 2–0, (A) 0–1; Zaire (A) 0–1, (H) 6–1; Morocco (A) 2–0, (H) 2–1.
Possible team: N'Kono – Kaham, Aoudo, Doumbe, M'Bow – Kunde, Abega, Tokoto – Bahoren, Milla, N'Guea.

I am sure Cameroon are going to come, see and be conquered when they step on to the World Cup finals stage for the first time. They will no doubt play above themselves but it will be a shock if they manage to take a single point off Italy, Poland or Peru. Cameroon follow Zaire as only the second Black African finalists and the moment New Zealand qualified there were the inevitable political rumours that the Africans would withdraw in protest.

Roger Milla, a powerful striker, is the star of the Cameroon attack and plays in France for the French Cup holders Bastia. Fluent and fast as Milla is, I don't think he is going to have the necessary support to help him find a way through world-class defences. What I've seen of the Cameroon team on film suggests they rely very heavily on goalkeeper Henry N'Kono, who is both agile and daring. He is going to have plenty of opportunities to show his spectacular skills in Spain. Cameroon are managed by Yugoslav coach Branko Zutic, a much-travelled man who knows the international football circuit well. He talks highly of the standard of club football in the Cameroons and this is born out by the fact that Cameroon clubs dominate the African league and cup competitions. But the World Cup is a different ball game altogether and I don't think they will be staying in Spain for very long. I recall that Zaire conceded 14 goals without netting one themselves in the 1974 finals. It's unlikely that Cameroon will fare much better.

Rating: 2**

ROGER MILLA, the jewel of the Cameroon attack.

Group 2

WEST GERMANY

Colours: White shirts/black shorts
Manager: Jupp Derwall
Qualifying results: Bulgaria (A) 3–1, (H) 4–0; Albania (A) 2–0, (H) 8–0; Austria (H) 2–0, (A) 3–1; Finland (A) 4–0, (H) 7–1.
Possible team: Schumacher – Kaltz, Stielike, K. H. Förster, Briegel – Dremmler, Breitner, H. Müller – Littbarski, Fischer, Rummenigge.

Played eight, won eight, goals for 33, against three – statistics that tell their own story of West Germany's devastating form in their World Cup qualifying matches. In fact the Germans have never lost a qualifying match since first entering World Cup competition back in 1934. They have the players and the plans to go all the way through to the World Cup final as Europe's strongest challengers. There is not a single weakness in the team and they have flair to go with their superb organisation.

Veteran Paul Breitner, now operating as midfield anchorman, is an inspiring captain and in Karl-Heinz Rummenigge the Germans have a player who could rival even the outstanding South American ball jugglers as the most effective forward in the tournament. The 1981 European Footballer of the Year is deadly when on the ball and can pull defences apart with his clever decoy runs when he shows a marvellous positional sense. The Germans have a draw that should not tax too much of their energy in the early matches and I expect them to be fresh and strong for the second stage of the competition when they could launch themselves all the way through to the Final and, possibly, the World Cup for a third time. I am sure they can avenge the surprise defeat by Austria in Argentina four years ago and I sense their biggest trouble in the group matches could come from Chile.

Rating: 9*******

KARL-HEINZ RUMMENIGGE . . . European Footballer of the Year.

Group 2

AUSTRIA

Colours: White shirts/black shorts
Manager: Karl Stotz
Qualifying results: Finland (A) 2–0, (H) 5–1; Albania (H) 5–0, (A) 1–0; West Germany (A) 0–2, (H) 1–3; Bulgaria (H) 2–0, (A) 0–0.
Possible team: Feurer – Krauss, Weber, Pezzey, Mirnegg – Prohaska, Hintermaier, Hattenberger, Jara – Krankl, Schachner.

Austria were twice badly mangled by the West German machine in their qualifying matches and cannot be looking forward to the task of meeting them again in Spain. I think it is going to be touch and go whether Austria or Chile join West Germany in the second stage of the competition. On their day, the Austrians can be a match for any team in the world, particularly when the gifted Hans Krankl is firing on all cylinders. But I have heard stories of unrest in the Austrian camp because of jealousies caused by the many 'exile' players in the squad earning fortunes abroad and coming home only for the matches that matter. Indeed, Austrian Football Federation President Karl Sekanina was moved to writing a personal letter to each member of the international squad reminding them of their responsibility to the team, to Austria and to their supporters. Having to be asked in writing to give 100 per cent for your team does not exactly encourage confidence in Austria's chances of surviving to the late stages of the competition.

If manager Karl Stotz can inject team spirit in the short time that he is going to have all his star players available to him once they are freed from club commitments, then Austria could be a side to watch. They have inventive and imaginative footballers who play with skill and flair. But the question that will not be answered until the finals kick off in June is whether they can get it together as a team. Their opening game against Chile on June 17 is crucial to both sides. That's when all the questions will be asked and answered.

Rating: 7*****

HANS KRANKL, the star of the Austrian camp.

HEIZUN

Group 2

CHILE

Colours: Red shirts/blue shorts
Manager: Luis Santibanez
Qualifying results: Ecuador (A) 0–0, (H) 2–0; Paraguay (A) 1–0, (H) 3–0.
Possible team: Osben – Garrido, Figueroa, Soto, Bigorra – Rojas, Neira, Dubo – Yanez, Caszely, Moscoso.

Even the all-powerful Germans will approach their match with Chile warily. They were comfortable winners of their qualifying group despite the presence of the then reigning South American champions Paraguay and just might prove the surprise packet of the tournament. Manager Luis Santibanez took charge of the team in 1977 and in their first game under his command Chile were beaten 4–2 by Scotland in Santiago. Chile have since improved out of sight and include draws with world champions Argentina and Spain in an impressive sequence of results. Their strength lies in the ability to mount quick counter attacks from a springboard of an unyielding defence in which the veteran Elias Figuero continues to reveal the form that has three times earned him the South American Footballer of the Year title and a high rating in the North American League where he now operates. I will resist the temptation to make any Irish-type jokes about their accomplished left-back Bigorra and move on to their attack which can give the tightest defences trouble. Among the forwards to watch out for are Carlos Caszely, a central striker who was a formidable force in Spain with Levante and Espanol, and jet-paced wingers Patricio Yanez and Gustavo Moscoso.

Much depends on whether the Chileans can adapt their game to European conditions. If they can reproduce their home form in Spain, there's every chance that they will go through to the second stage of the tournament with West Germany. The fact that they did not concede a single goal in their four qualifying matches will strike fear into the hearts of their opponents. It just might be Chile's year for making a big impact on world football.

Rating: 8******

CARLOS CASZELY, Chile's formidable striker.

Group 2

ALGERIA

Colours: Green shirts/white shorts
Manager: Yevgeni Rogov
Qualifying results: Sierra Leone (A) 2–2, (H) 3–1; Sudan (H) 2–0, (A) 1–1; Niger (H) 4–0, (A) 0–1; Nigeria (A) 2–0, (H) 2–1.
Possible team: Cerbah – Larbes, Kourichi, Guendouz, Mansouri – Kaci Said, Mayouz, Belloumi – Madjer, Zidane, Dahleb.

Algeria are unlikely to play more than a walk-on part in their first appearance in the World Cup finals. Their Russian coach Yevgeni Rogov has introduced discipline and organisation into their team play but they just do not have the individual skill and technique to hope to be able to live with the powerful opposition they will meet in Spain. They have never before managed to get past the second round in the African qualifying tournament and surpassed and surprised themselves by beating Nigeria home and away to clinch a place in Spain. Their team is strongly influenced by players who have widened their experience and tactical knowledge with action in the French league. Two of these – defender Nordine Kourichi and striker Mustafa Dahleb – are top-quality footballers but it takes more than two men to make a team at World Cup level. Another player the Algerians expect a lot from is support striker Lakhdar Belloumi who scored two crucial goals in the matches against Nigeria. But he lacks consistency and has never played against the sort of redoubtable defences that will be marshalled against him when he faces West Germany, Austria and Chile. An indication of the rising power of the Algerians is that Jet of Tizi-Ouzo – one of their top club sides – beat Vita of Zaire in the African Champions' Cup. The game is flourishing in Algeria but they are still a long way off what passes for world-class and I will be astonished if they register a win in Spain.

Rating: 3★★★

NORDINE KOURICHI of Algeria – 'top quality'.

DIEGO MARADONA . . . a marked man.

Group 3

ARGENTINA

Colours: Blue and white striped shirts/black shorts
Manager: Cesar Luis Menotti
Qualify as reigning champions.
Possible team: Fillol – Olguin, Galvan, Passarella, Tarantini – Ardiles, Gallego, Maradona – Amuchastegui, Ramon Diaz, Kempes.

Any team that has the magic of Maradona, the artistry of Ardiles and the 'killer' touch of Kempes must be rated as potential Cup winners. There is no doubt that Argentina have the ammunition to retain the trophy they won in such style back home in Buenos Aires four years ago. My only apprehension about tipping them for a place in the Final is because of their suspect temperament. If they can show the discipline that was an important part of their success in 1978, then even the Brazilians and West Germans will be hard pressed to hold them. But they are not going to get the favours from the referees that was evident in Argentina when they had that vast crowd noisily on their side. How will they react when decisions go against them? What will their morale be like if things don't go their way right from the first kick? They have been drawn in a group that should not provide too many problems and they could easily get into a winning rhythm that will take them all the way into the Final. But my doubts are based on experience of playing against Argentinians and watching them at close quarters in many matches. That great ambassador Osvaldo Ardiles should give all his team-mates lessons in how to react in a sporting, gracious manner when a referee's decision is not what they expected.

I have heard many different stories about whether Maradona will actually deign to play in Spain. He will be a marked man when he – as I'm sure he will – decides to join the greatest soccer show on earth. Maradona has the skill to take over the World Cup stage. If he can produce just glimpses of his best form, everybody is in for a treat except defences that are on the receiving end.

Rating: 9*******

\ race for possession between Holland's Krol and .uque of Argentina in the 1978 Final.

Group 3

BELGIUM

Colours: All white
Manager: Guy Thys
Qualifying results: Eire (A) 1–1, (H) 1–0; Holland (H) 1–0, (A) 0–3; Cyprus (A) 2–0, (H) 3–2; France (A) 2–3, (H) 2–0.
Possible team: Pfaff – Gerets, Meeuws, Millecamps, Renquin – Vandereycken, Van Moer, Van der Elst, Lozano – Vandenbergh, Ceulemans.

Belgium were the first European team to qualify for the finals from a difficult group and need to be treated with respect. They have several young players pressing for consideration and by the time the finals kick off in Spain it could be that 21-year-old striker Alex Czerniatynski will have forced his way into the attack. The son of a Polish immigrant miner, he has made rapid progress since joining Royal Antwerp from Charleroi and it was his debut goal against France that helped clinch Belgium's ticket to Spain. Another bonus for the Belgians is that Spanish-born midfielder Juan Lozano has been naturalised in time to be included in their World Cup squad. He has been outstanding with Anderlecht.

The issue that has been the talk of Belgium is whether veteran midfield schemer Wilfried Van Moer can be persuaded to change his mind about retiring from international football and lead his country's challenge for the World Cup. This will be a vital factor because without Van Moer's driving power, Belgium's chances of making an impact will be greatly reduced. The Belgians are well organised and have married good individual skills to sound teamwork. They are very competitive players and manager Guy Thys has got them working to a team pattern that is going to make them difficult to beat. I doubt if they will make it as far as the semi-finals but they could give several of the more fancied teams some nasty shocks before the final shots of the 1982 tournament have been fired. If they can reproduce the form that took them to second place in the 1980 European championships, Belgium could really sparkle in Spain.

Rating: 7*****

RAYMOND MOMMENS of Belgium heads for goal against West Germany.

Group 3

HUNGARY

Colours: Red shirts/white shorts
Manager: Kalman Meszoly
Qualifying results: Switzerland (A) 2–2, (H) 3–0; Rumania (H) 1–0, (A) 0–0; Norway (A) 2–1, (H) 4–1; England (H) 1–3, (A) 0–1.
Possible team: Meszaros – Martos, Balint, Kerekes, Toth – Sallai, Muller, Nyilasi – Fazekas, Torocsik, Kiss.

Which Hungarian team will we see in Spain? The one that scored vital victories over Switzerland, Norway and Rumania when it really mattered, or the one that tamely surrendered to England at Wembley after they had made certain of qualifying for the finals? Like all Hungarian teams since the 1950s, they are haunted by ghosts past from the days of the Magical Magyars. Nothing I've seen from the current Hungarian team suggests they can begin to live with the reputations and exploits of the magnificent Puskas-Kocsis-Hidegkuti side.

In Nyilasi and Torocsik, the Hungarians have two players with the ability to trouble any defence but their application is sometimes suspect. I recall them both getting sent off in a bad-tempered match against Argentina in the 1978 finals. Their temperaments will be put to the test when they face the Argentinians again in Alicante on June 18. Watch out for fireworks! I have been disappointed in the team performances of Hungary when they have been in action against England in recent years. They seem to lack co-ordination and consistency. It will be as much as I expect from them if they can survive to the second stage of the competition but they could prove me wrong in my estimation if they can reproduce the fire and flair they showed when taking three points from Rumania, three from Switzerland and maximum points from the Norwegians. It was a better qualifying record than England managed.

Rating: 7*****

KEVIN KEEGAN challenges for a '50–50' ball against Hungary.

Group 3

EL SALVADOR

Colours: All blue
Manager: Mauricio Rodriguez
Qualifying results *(their last five matches were played in a tournament in Honduras)*: Panama (A) 3–1, (H) 4–1; Costa Rica (H) 2–0, (A) 0–0; Guatemala (A) 0–0, (H) 1–0; Honduras (H) 2–1, (A) 0–2, (A) 0–0; Canada (A) 0–1; Mexico (A) 1–0; Cuba (A) 0–0; Haiti (A) 1–0.
Possible team: Guevara – Becinos, Jovel, Osorio, Diaz – Ventura, Alfaro, Huezo – Montoya, Nunez, Gonzalez.

El Salvador finished runners-up in their qualifying group behind Honduras. These two Central American republics waged war against each other 12 years ago following a World Cup qualifying clash and they have hardly been the best of neighbours ever since. I am positive we will be spared the sight of them continuing their feud in Spain because the chances of either team surviving their group matches are next to nil.

Don't expect El Salvador to bring spectators to the edge of their seats with their play in Spain. They are heavily biased towards defence as was proved in their five qualifying tournament matches in Honduras when they scored just two goals and conceded one. They have three key players – goalkeeper Luis Ricardo Guevara, captain and midfield organiser Jose Norberto Huezo and striker Jorge Alberto Gonzalez, who has been described (loosely I suspect) as the 'Maradona of Central America'. If comparisons are to be made, I think we will find Jose Norberto Huezo similar in style to a dear old favourite of mine. He apparently tries to cover every inch of ground in midfield and tackles like a train. Shades of one Norbert (Nobby) Stiles! El Salvador are proud of their defiant defence. I believe it is going to be well drilled before the Group 3 matches are over.

Rating: 4★★★★

JOSE HUEZO, Captain of El Salvador, in action during a qualifying match against Haiti.

Group 4

ENGLAND

Colours: White shirts/royal blue shorts
Manager: Ron Greenwood
Qualifying results: Norman (H) 4–0, (A) 1–2; Romania (A) 1–2, (H) 0–0; Switzerland (H) 2–1, (A) 1–2; Hungary (A) 3–1, (H) 1–0.
Possible team *(based on Ron Greenwood's thinking rather than mine)*: Clemence – Neal, Thompson, Martin, Mills – Wilkins, McDermott, Robson, Brooking – Keegan, Mariner

There was nothing in England's spluttering form in the qualifying matches to inspire confidence, yet I have an old pro's gut feeling that they could be one of the sensations of the tournament in Spain. I don't think they have the ability to go all the way and emulate Alf Ramsey's 1966 team but I sense that a semi-final place is not beyond them. If I were in Ron Greenwood's place I would be going big on the skill factor, drafting in players like Glenn Hoddle, Cyrille Regis and Tony Morley to bring flair into the attack.

England are the luckiest team in the world to be through to the finals and have Switzerland to thank rather than their own efforts. Yet all past form goes out of the window once the World Cup kicks off and, provided he gets the right mix between youth and experience, Greenwood could find himself hailed as the manager of the tournament. That wouldn't be bad considering how many people were shouting for his head after England's humiliating defeat in Norway. It's my personal view that Peter Shilton is the superior goalkeeper to Ray Clemence and he would be my choice to play in the opening match against France in Bilbao on June 16. My England team for Spain (please bear in mind that I am making this selection before Greenwood has named his squad of 40 players) would be: Shilton – Thomas, Robson, Foster, Statham – Keegan, McDermott, Hoddle – Francis, Regis, Morley.

I doubt if Greenwood will be this bold. In my opinion, Bryan Robson is a more effective force as a central defender where his combination of power and skill will mean England will be playing football from the back. Accurate passing is going to be vital in Spain where the heat, even in late evening, can drain the stamina out of the fittest players.

Rating: 8********

KEVIN KEEGAN . . . England's captain puts the Hungarian defence under pressure.

Group 4

FRANCE

Colours: Blue shirts/white shorts
Manager: Michel Hidalgo
Qualifying results: Cyprus (A) 7–0, (H) 4–0; Eire (H) 2–0, (A) 2–3; Belgium (H) 3–2, (A) 2–0; Holland (A) 0–1, (H) 2–0.
Possible team: Castaneda – Janvion, Lopez, Tresor, Bossis – Giresse, Platini, Genghini – Rocheteau, Lacombe, Six.

England will be quickly able to gauge their chances of progressing to the second stage of the finals when they face the formidable French team in the opening match of Group 4 on June 16. If they can overcome the French – as England did in the 1966 Finals when I played my last World Cup match – then it will give them the impetus for a successful run. But it's not going to be easy. The French are inconsistent but when they are getting it all together they can be an exceptional side. I considered them the unluckiest of all the teams in the 1978 finals when they were pipped in exciting matches by Argentina and Italy. Either game could easily have gone to France if they'd had luck to match their output.

In Michel Platini, the French have one of the most imaginative midfield players in the world. He will need close attention and England must beware his free-kicks that come swerving in Brazilian fashion. France have already revealed their quality by coming through a tough qualifying group in which they had to battle with Eire, Belgium and Holland. Their survival is a testimony to their talent. They have a world-class defender in Marius Tresor and Rocheteau, Lacombe and Six make up a front-line trio that can dismantle the strongest defences. A tendency to lose concentration and heart when the going gets really tough is all that prevents France from getting a higher star rating. If they kick off with a victory against England, the French could set fire to all predictions.

Rating: 7*****

MICHEL PLATINI, France's imaginative midfield player.

Group 4

CZECHOSLOVAKIA

Colours: Red shirts/white shorts
Manager: Josef Venglos
Qualifying results: Wales (A) 0–1, (H) 2–0; Turkey (H) 2–0, (A) 3–0; Iceland (H) 6–1, (A) 1–1; Russia (A) 0–2, (H) 1–1.
Possible team: Hruska – Jakubec, Vojacek, Fiala, Barmos – Berger, Panenka, Stambachr, Jurkemik – Masny, Nehoda.

The Czechs have qualified for Spain with an ageing but wily team of campaigners. They are still a match for the best teams in the world but I have a feeling that old legs are going to start to drag after an hour or so of hard toil in what is always an energy-draining competition even in kinder climates. Manager Josef Venglos was talking optimistically of introducing fresh faces before the summer finals but it's more than likely that when the crunch comes he will rely on tried and trusted players. If plundering partners Marian Masny and Zdenek Nehoda can capture their best form, then no defence in the tournament is safe under attack from this dynamic duo. I reckon, however, that they have left their best behind them and that Czechoslovakia are not the force they were when winning the European championship. They have a class player in midfield in Panenka who can pull defences apart with precision-placed passes. Here again, though, age could be the anchor. Panenka is coming up 34 and I doubt if he can sustain his driving enthusiasm over a quick succession of punishing matches. Josef Venglos is a dedicated and knowledgeable football coach who shares Ron Greenwood's devotion to the theory and technique of the game. He will have ambitious plans prepared for his players but will they have the stamina to carry them out? The Czechs are going to find it very hard work but it would be foolish to dismiss them. Old engines can often be souped up to outspeed new machines.

Rating: 7*****

MARIAN MASNY . . . causing problems to the West German defence.

Group 4

KUWAIT

Colours: Blue shirts/white shorts
Manager: Carlos Alberto Parreira
Qualifying results: Thailand (H) 6–0; Malaysia (H) 4–0; South Korea (H) 2–0; New Zealand (A) 2–1, (H) 2–2; China 0–3, (H) 1–0; Saudi Arabia (A) 1–0, (H) 2–0.

Kuwait have only 1,638 registered players among their population of one million, so their feat in reaching the World Cup finals is quite phenomenal. If there is a 'North Korea' lurking in the tournament, then it just might be these Arabs who play a fair standard of football which is a credit to their Brazilian coach Carlos Alberto Parreira (*not*, incidentally, the same Carlos Alberto as captained the 1970 World Cup winning Brazilians).

I'm grateful to my old Spurs chum Dave 'King' Mackay for giving background information on the strength of Kuwait. Dave, who has won great respect as a coach in the Middle East, reports: 'Nobody should under-estimate Kuwait. Six of their international squad play for my club side and they have the skill and the enthusiasm to compete at top level. They don't have powerful phsysiques yet are strong on the ball and determined in the tackle. Two to watch out for in particular are midfield partners Abdulla Bluchy and Mohammed Karem. They are tireless workers who can take charge of a match if given half a chance. Abdulla, who is serving in the Army at the moment, has a long-range shot that is as powerful as any I've seen.'

I think Kuwait will struggle to settle to European conditions but their pride and enthusiasm could lift them into producing the sort of shocks that light up most World Cup tournaments. But looking at it realistically, I cannot see them getting past the first stage. Their spirit will be willing but I think their tactical knowledge at this level will be weak.

Rating: 5*****

ABDUL AZIZ AL ANBARI . . . a key man for Kuwait.

Group 5

SPAIN

Colours: Red shirts/blue shorts
Manager: Jose Santamaria
Qualify as host country.
Possible team: Arconada – Camacho, Tendillo, Alesanco, Gordillo – Victor, Miguel Alonso, Zamora – Juanito, Santillana, Lopez Ufarte.

There has rarely been a World Cup tournament in which the host country has not made a big impact. In fact three of the last four finals have been won by the home country: England (1966), West Germany (1974) and Argentina (1978). Spain have every chance because the draw has been kind to them but I think they will struggle to reach the last four. It is no secret that the atmosphere in the Spanish camp has been poisoned by disputes between rival sets of players and manager Jose Santamaria, one-time Uruguay, Spain and Real Madrid centre-half, has got it all to do to mould the team into a winning unit. I remember the hidden success factor for England in 1966 was the club atmosphere that Alf Ramsey managed to introduce at international level. This must be Santamaria's aim if he is to get the best out of his talented but temperamental players.

Spain have been playing an average game a month for the last 18 months in a bid to find the right blend and balance. Real Madrid striker Juanito is their most dangerous player and Santamaria risked a lynching when he dropped him following a loss of form. If Juanito is at the peak of his power at the right time and if Zamora is allowed room to manoeuvre in midfield – and if the team spirit is right – then Spain, with massive crowds to lift them, could be happy and successful hosts. But there are a lot of 'ifs' about a team that can be brilliant or brittle, according to their mood of the moment. One thing's for sure, they won't be boring.

Rating: 8*********

JESUS ZAMORA . . . taking a tumble against England goalkeeper Ray Clemence.

Group 5

HONDURAS

Colours: Blue shirts/white shorts
Manager: Chelato Herrera
Qualifying results: Panama (A) 2–0, (H)5–0; Costa Rica (A) 3–2, (H) 1–1; Guatemala (H) 0–0, (A) 1–0; El Salvador (A) 1–2, (H) 2–0; Haiti (H) 4–0; Cuba (H) 2–0; Canada (H) 2–1; Mexico (H) 0–0.
Possible team: Arzu – Guttierez, Costly, Villegas, Buines – Zelaya, Maradiaga, Buesco – Urquia, Bailey, Figueroa.

It is unlikely that Honduras will take much more than a passing interest in their first venture into the World Cup final stages. They won their Central American group in impressive style but the opposition was second-rate compared with what they will come up against in Spain. Their manager Chelato Herrera has got them well organised during a two-year build up for this, the greatest moment in their football history. They have three fast and flashy forwards in Roberto Figueroa, Jorge Urquia, and Jimmy Bailey, who first emerged as a rising young star in the 1979 World Youth Cup. The man who does most to make the team tick is skipper Ramon Maradiaga, who plays an all-purposes role in mid-field. I am told by Canadian contacts who watched the qualifying tournament in Honduras: 'Stop Maradiaga from playing and you stop Honduras'. The defence is held together by Costly 'Senior', a solid and uncompromising centre-back whose brother – Costly 'Junior' – is likely to be in the squad as a reserve striker.

Honduras have the unenviable job of tackling hosts Spain in their first match in Valencia on June 16. I would not give a 1978 World Cup Final ticket for their chances of winning and they just might take a tanking which will destroy their confidence for the rest of the tournament. There again, if they could scrape a draw with Spain . . .

Rating: 3***

RAMON MARADIAGA directing operations for Honduras.

Group 5

YUGOSLAVIA

Colours: blue shirts/white shorts
Manager: Miljan Miljanic
Qualifying results: Luxemburg (A) 5–0, (H) 5–0; Denmark (H) 2–1, (A) 2–1; Italy (A) 0–2, (H) 1–1; Greece (H) 5–1, (A) 2–1.
Possible team: Pantelic – Stojkovic, Zajec, Buljan, Gudelj – Zlato Vujovic, Zoran Vujovic, Petrovic, Surjak – Halilhodzic, Susic.

Miljan Miljanic will not kick a ball in Spain but could prove one of the most influential people in the tournament. He is the manager of Yugoslavia, a Svengali character who has a long history of producing winning tactics for his teams. Real Madrid and Red Star Belgrade are just two of the clubs that have benefited from his astonishing ability to motivate men into playing above themselves. He started plotting Yugoslavia's World Cup challenge two years ago and has brought his team nicely to the boil at the right time for the finals. They won their qualifying group ahead of Italy which gives an indication of their strength.

Miljanic has managed to get a pattern and plan running through his team despite having to patiently wait for many of his star players to return from commitments with overseas clubs. From what I've seen of Yugoslavia on film, they play football all the way from the back with their defenders always looking to use the ball constructively in neatly-operated counter attacks. I particularly like the positive play in midfield of skipper Ivo Surjak, who used to be an influential force with Hajduk Split before moving into the French league with Paris St Germain. If you're looking for a team that will give you a good run for your money at reasonable odds then Yugoslavia are a tempting side to follow. It will be interesting to see what happens if and when they are awarded a penalty. Their chief penalty taker in recent matches has been goalkeeper Dragan Pantelic. Yugoslavia are the best of the 'outsiders'.

Rating: 8*********

IVO SURJAK, Captain of Yugoslavia.

Group 5

NORTHERN IRELAND

Colours: Green shirts/white shorts
Manager: Billy Bingham
Qualifying results: Israel (A) 0–0, (H) 1–0; Sweden (H) 3–0, (A) 0–1; Portugal (A) 0–0, (H) 1–0; Scotland (A) 1–1, (H) 0–0.
Possible team: Jennings – J. Nicholl, C. Nicholl, J. O'Neill, Donaghy – M. O'Neill, McIlroy, McRory, McCreery – Brotherston, Armstrong, Hamilton.

One thing's for sure – no team will enjoy the World Cup finals as much as Northern Ireland. They will go there with a relaxed, all-to-gain-nothing-to-lose attitude and while, on paper, they look to have little hope of great success it could be a different story on the pitch. I recall them being written off before the 1958 Finals but they laughed and stylishly played their way through to the quarter-finals. Billy Bingham was a playing member of that team and I am sure that now, as manager, he will be trying to recreate the magical team spirit generated by footballing immortals like Danny Blanchflower, Jimmy McIlroy and Peter Doherty back in '58.

What has given me the greatest pleasure is to see that magnificent goalkeeper Pat Jennings at last get the world stage that he deserves. He is a marvellous ambassador for our game as well as being an exceptional player and with his big hands at the back of the defence Northern Ireland are always in with a chance regardless of the opposition. As much as I would love to witness a succession of Northern Ireland victories, the cold professional inside me insists that they do not have the all-round strength to get past the group opposition they are going to face against Spain and Yugoslavia. But one thing I am certain of is that the Northern Ireland players will win friends, with their football and their friendly attitude. Billy Bingham would not have it any other way.

Rating: 6*******

SAMMY McILROY . . . showing the sort of form he hopes to reveal for Northern Ireland in Spain. McIlroy's header is admired by his Manchester United team-mate Steve Coppell, a member of England's World Cup squad. McIlroy has since transferred to Stoke City . . . following in the path of his famous namesake Jimmy McIlroy, who starred for Northern Ireland in the 1958 World Cup finals.

Group 6

BRAZIL

Colours: Yellow shirts/blue shorts
Manager: Tele Santana
Qualifying matches: Venezuela (A) 1–0, (H) 5–0; Bolivia (A) 2–1, (H) 3–1.
Possible team: Valdir Peres – Edevaldo, Luisinho, Oscar, Junior – Toninho, Cerezo, Socrates, Falcao – Paulo Isidoro, Roberto, Zico.

Brazil are just about everybody's favourites for the title, including mine. We know they have the skill, we know they can win outside South America and we know that all the other teams in the tournament are frightened of them. Just think back to their last European tour when they took on England, France and West Germany and beat the lot of them. It wasn't just that they beat them but it was the *style* in which they achieved their victories. To me they looked to be potentially as good as the winning Brazilian teams of 1958, 1962 and 1970. And that means very, very good. Out of this world, in fact.

Yes, I'm expecting a lot from Brazil and I don't think I shall be disappointed. They have not got an easy group draw and I think that could work in their favour. Manager Tele Santana will really have them pumped up and if they win their tough opening game against Russia in Seville on June 14 then I don't believe anybody will be able to stop them. Anybody who saw the way Brazilian club champions Flamengo took Liverpool apart in the World Club Cup in Tokyo in December, 1981, will know that Brazil have players who might have come off another planet. They were light years ahead of Liverpool in thought and deed. I am particularly looking forward to seeing Zico parade his skills in Spain. He could prove the king of the tournament, even ahead of Maradona. I have heard doubts expressed about the merits of goalkeeper Valdir Peres but Brazil have often proved themselves the best in the world despite having goalkeepers with careless hands as a last line of defence. I just can't wait to see that Brazil–Russia opening match in Group 6. It could be the match of the tournament and possibly a preview of the Final.

Rating: 10**********

A jubilant PELE scores Brazil's first goal in their 4–1 victory over Italy, 1970.

ZICO . . . he could be the King in Spain.

Group 6

RUSSIA

Colours: Red shirts/white shorts
Manager: Konstantin Beskov
Qualifying results: Iceland (H) 5–0, (A) 2–1; Wales (A) 0–0, (H) 3–0; Turkey (H) 4–0, (A) 3–0; Czechoslovakia (H) 2–0, (A) 1–1.
Possible team: Dassayev – Sulakvelidze, Chivadze, Baltacha, Burovsky – Daraselia, Butyak, Bessonov – Shengelia, Gavrilov, Blokhin.

Russia have had a habit in the past of promising more than they produce in World Cup competition but this year they could deliver in style. Gone is the 'Red Robot' image of previous Russian teams. Manager Konstantin Beskov has achieved his objective of marrying flair with the traditional Soviet discipline and the result is a national team that stands a chance against the best in Spain. The side will include at least four of the Dynamo Tblisi team that destroyed West Ham with a pulverising performance in the European Cup Winners' Cup at Upton Park in 1981. I saw that display and thought then that Russia could be a devastating force in Spain if they could show anything approaching this form. The players that impressed me included David Kipiani, Sulakvelidze, Chivadze, Daraselia and Shengelia, all of whom are regular members of the Russian squad (although Kipiani's progress was halted by a broken leg).

Beskov has moulded these gifted individual players into an exciting side that, as Welsh team manager Mike England will confirm, can be very competitive as well as spectacular. *The* player to watch for is Kiev outside-left Oleg Blokhin who can destroy any defence when at full throttle. He is the nearest I have seen to one of my boyhood heroes, Tom Finney. I cannot give him higher praise than that. I will be surprised if the Russians don't at least make it to the semi-finals. Then wait for the bidding to start for Blokhin, who is going to be allowed to export his skills to the West once the World Cup shooting and shouting is over.

Rating: 9*******

Russia's Kipiani . . . victim of a broken leg.

CCCP

Group 6

SCOTLAND

Colours: Dark blue shirts/white shorts
Manager: Jock Stein
Qualifying results: Sweden (A) 1–0, (H) 2–0; Portugal (H) 0–0, (A) 1–2; Israel (A) 1–0, (H) 3–1; Northern Ireland (H) 1–1, (A) 0–0.
Possible team: Rough – McGrain, Miller, Hansen, E. Gray – Strachan, Souness, Hartford – Dalglish, Jordan, Robertson.

Scotland were treated really harshly by a World Cup draw that pitches them into the same group as Brazil and Russia, the two teams they would most wanted to have avoided. Their astute manager Jock Stein will need to produce some sort of tactical wizardry if the Scots are to survive to the second stage of the competition. They will be hoping that Russia and Brazil don't draw in their opening encounter. Then they must try to squeeze a point out of each of them after going all out for a cricket score against New Zealand in their opening group match on June 15 in Malaga.

I am at least confident that the Scots will wipe out the nightmare memories of Argentina. Stein has wisely insisted on a low-key build-up to the finals and their supporters will not be expecting too much of them. So any points gained will be a bonus.

Maybe I'm under-estimating Scotland and over-estimating the Brazilians and Russians. My heart wants Scotland to do well but my head tells me they are going to make an early journey home even though in players like Danny McGrain, Graeme Souness, Kenny Dalglish and John Robertson they have footballers of the highest calibre. At least Stein and his men know the size of the mountain they have to climb and there will not be the complacency and over confidence that led them into so much trouble and embarrassment in Argentina.

Rating: 7*****

JOE JORDAN . . . Scotland's Italian-based centre-forward releases the ball under strong pressure from England centre-half Dave Watson.

Group 6

NEW ZEALAND

Colours: White shirts/black shorts
Manager: John Ashmead
Qualifying results: Australia (H) 3–3, (A) 2–0; Fiji (A) 4–0, (H) 13–0; Taiwan (A) 0–0, (H) 2–0; Indonesia (A) 2–0, (H) 5–0; China (A) 0–0, (H) 1–0; Kuwait (H) 1–2, (A) 2–2; Saudi Arabia (H) 2–2, (A) 5–0; Beat China 2–1 in a play-off.
Possible team: Wilson – Hill, Herbert, Almond, Elrick – Mackay, Sumner, Cole, Turner – Woofer, Wooddin.

It's good to see our cousins from Down Under qualifying for the World Cup finals for the first time. They have already written World Cup history by notching up a record score of 13–0 when beating Fiji during their marathon qualifying serial that finally ended in triumph with a 2–1 victory over China in a dramatic play-off match. That's all the good news. Now the bad. I'm afraid they are coming a long, long way for a triple thrashing. I just cannot see how they are going to escape hammerings by Scotland, Russia and then Brazil in the toughest group in the tournament.

New Zealand set up an impressive sequence of victories coming into 1982, losing only one of 19 international matches. But they have been playing against strictly second-class opposition when compared with world giants Brazil and Russia and the very capable Scots. Managed by John Ashmead and coached by Rotherham-born Kevin Fallon, the Kiwis are determined to put on a display that will give football a boost in Rugby-conscious New Zealand. I hope for their sake I'm proved wrong but I sense they will rue the day they qualified for the finals. All I can say to cheer New Zealand supporters up is that I am sure there were alleged experts making similar noises about North Korea in 1966. And look what they achieved.

Rating: 4*****

New Zealand's STEVE SUMNER and McKAY in action against Kuwait.

THE WORLD CUP DIARY

DATE	VENUE	GROUP	TEAMS
June 13 (Sunday)	Barcelona	Three	Argentina v Belgium
June 14 (Monday)	Vigo Seville	One Six	Italy v Poland Brazil v Soviet Union
June 15 (Tuesday)	La Coruna Elche Malaga	One Three Six	Peru v Cameroon Hungary v El Salvador Scotland v New Zealand
June 16 (Wednesday)	Gijon Bilbao Valencia	Two Four Five	W. Germany v Algeria England v France Spain v Honduras
June 17 (Thursday)	Oviedo Valladolid Zaragoza	Two Four Five	Chile v Austria Czechoslovakia v Kuwait Yugoslavia v N. Ireland
June 18 (Friday)	Vigo Alicante Seville	One Three Six	Italy v Peru Argentina v Hungary Brazil v Scotland
June 19 (Saturday)	La Coruna Elche Malaga	One Three Six	Poland v Cameroon Belgium v El Salvador Soviet Union v New Zealand
June 20 (Sunday)	Gijon Bilbao Valencia	Two Four Five	W. Germany v Chile England v Czechoslovakia Spain v Yugoslavia
June 21 (Monday)	Oviedo Valladolid Zaragoza	Two Four Five	Algeria v Austria France v Kuwait Honduras v N. Ireland
June 22 (Tuesday)	La Coruna Elche Malaga	One Three Six	Peru v Poland Belgium v Hungary Soviet Union v Scotland
June 23 (Wednesday)	Vigo Alicante Seville	One Three Six	Italy v Cameroon Argentina v El Salvador Brazil v New Zealand
June 24 (Thursday)	Oviedo Valladolid Zaragoza	Two Four Five	Algeria v Chile France v Czechoslovakia Honduras v Yugoslavia
June 25 (Friday)	Gijon Bilbao Valencia	Two Four Five	W. Germany v Austria England v Kuwait N. Ireland v Spain

RESULTS

The twelve teams qualifying from the first round will be divided into four groups of three :

GROUP A: Winners of Group 1, winners of Group 3, runners-up of Group 6
GROUP B: Winners of Group 2, winners of Group 4, runners-up of Group 5
GROUP C: Winners of Group 6, runners-up of Group 1, runners-up of Group 3
GROUP D: Winners of Group 5, runners-up of Group 2, runners-up of Group 4

RESULT	GROUP ONE			RESULT
	Italy	v	Poland	
	Peru	v	Cameroon	
	Italy	v	Peru	
	Poland	v	Cameroon	
	Peru	v	Poland	
	Italy	v	Cameroon	

	GROUP TWO			
	W. Germany	v	Algeria	
	Chile	v	Austria	
	W. Germany	v	Chile	
	Algeria	v	Austria	
	Algeria	v	Chile	
	W. Germany	v	Austria	

	GROUP THREE			
	Argentina	v	Belgium	
	Hungary	v	El Salvador	
	Argentina	v	Hungary	
	Belgium	v	Hungary	
	Belgium	v	El Salvador	
	Argentina	v	El Salvador	

RESULT	GROUP FOUR			RESULT
	England	v	France	
	Czechoslovakia	v	Kuwait	
	England	v	Czechoslovakia	
	France	v	Kuwait	
	France	v	Czechoslovakia	
	England	v	Kuwait	

	GROUP FIVE			
	Spain	v	Honduras	
	Yugoslavia	v	N. Ireland	
	Spain	v	Yugoslavia	
	Honduras	v	N. Ireland	
	Honduras	v	Yugoslavia	
	N. Ireland	v	Spain	

	GROUP SIX			
	Brazil	v	Soviet Union	
	Scotland	v	New Zealand	
	Brazil	v	Scotland	
	Soviet Union	v	New Zealand	
	Soviet Union	v	Scotland	
	Brazil	v	New Zealand	

Barcelona and Madrid from June 28 - July 5
Group winners qualify for semi-finals

RESULT	TEAM	GROUP A	TEAM	RESULT
		V		
		V		
		V		

		GROUP B		
		V		
		V		
		V		

		GROUP C		
		V		
		V		
		V		

		GROUP D		
		V		
		V		
		V		

SEMI-FINALS

Barcelona and Seville on July 8

		V		
		V		

FINAL

Madrid, on July 11

		V		

ACKNOWLEDGEMENTS

The research work of the authors was made considerably easier by being able to refer to the magnificent *History of the World Cup* by *Sunday Times* football correspondent Brian Glanville, whose knowledge of the international soccer scene is unsurpassed. The authors would also like to acknowledge the monthly magazine *World Soccer*, which is always packed with information and news on international football wherever it is played; also top statistician Jack Rollin, Editor of the *Guinness Book of Soccer Feats* and the irreplaceable *Rothman's Football Year Book*.

Photographs kindly provided by Syndication International, Central Press, the Keystone Press Agency, Bob Thomas Sports Photography, and the New Zealand High Commission.

Picture research by Malcolm Rowley.